RANGERS

THE JOURNEY PART 1

The SFL 3 trophy takes pride of place in the Ibrox trophy room. It may not have the same importance
as the Glasgow Cup and European Cup Winners' Cup (right) but it will hold a place in Rangers' history.

RANGERS

THE JOURNEY PART 1

THE ILLUSTRATED STORY OF THE 2012/13 SEASON

Lindsay Herron

Photography by Kirk O'Rourke

BLACK & WHITE PUBLISHING

First published 2013
by Black & White Publishing Ltd
29 Ocean Drive, Edinburgh EH6 6JL

1 3 5 7 9 10 8 6 4 2   13 14 15 16

ISBN: 978 1 84502 714 8

Design by Stuart Polson Design
Printed and bound by in Poland
www.hussarbooks.pl

Contents

Introduction   vii

1   Turmoil, Turbulence and Takeover   1

2   Recruitment and Record Breaking   15

3   Cup Highs and Lows   29

4   Share of the Spoils   43

5   Return of a Legend   55

6   December Will Be Magic   67

7   New Year Blues   85

8   Sporting Integrity Intact   99

9   Slow March to the Title   111

10   All Change at the Top   125

11   Silver Lining   139

Acknowledgements

I would like to thank Ally McCoist and his coaches and players for their great co-operation in making this book possible by allowing unprecedented access during such an often turbulent season in SFL 3.

The resilience of the coaching staff and the players has been remarkable considering all they have had to put up with in the first part of the journey back to the top of the Scottish game.

There was great pressure coming from all angles but they found time to be available and to co-operate with all of the Rangers media team, and for that I am truly grateful.

Lindsay Herron

Introduction

RANGERS is a name that resonates in world football for the incredible successes and achievements, great players and great managers, stunning trophy haul and remarkable support. However, this great institution which affects the lives of so many almost ceased to be in the spring of 2012 when the club plunged into administration as a result of the disastrous tenure of Craig Whyte.

Many supporters feared they may never see their team again as the 2011/12 season drew to a close and different consortia made efforts to try to take control of the club. However, it has been the supporters who have ensured the continued life of Rangers and the remarkable recovery in the 2012/13 season. They rallied magnificently in the months of administration by filling out Ibrox and contributing to the Rangers Fans' Fighting Fund, and then stunned the global game as they set world record attendances and over 38,000 season tickets were sold.

It was Charles Green and his consortium who completed a deal for the club on 13 May 2012 and he faced incredible hurdles over a turbulent summer to not only secure Rangers' survival, but ensure there was a future. However, even he would not last the season as he stepped down as chief executive over press reports linking him with Whyte, which were damaging to the club.

Crushingly, Her Majesty's Revenue and Customs refused to support an exit from administration through a Company Voluntary Arrangement, which would have meant a 'pence in the pound' deal for creditors. This led to Green forming a new company and transferring the assets, honours and history from the old company, which would go into a liquidation process.

The formation of a 'newco' is something that has happened on a number of occasions in English football and has been dealt with in a calm and business-like manner. In Scotland, it seemed that mass hysteria broke out. There was bitterness and rancour in the air and Rangers had few friends, if any, it seemed, as they tried to get back on their feet. The phrase 'sporting integrity' became the misnomer of the year as the other clubs clung to it as a reason for not supporting Rangers getting back into the SPL under their new ownership. It was a fiasco as the SPL then tried to force the SFL into taking Rangers into the First Division, which they refused to do, and at the end of it all the Light Blues were plunged into the fourth tier of the game.

So a new journey for Rangers was to begin in SFL 3, taking them to places like Elgin and Peterhead, Annan and Berwick and Stirling and Montrose, but not before the club was forced to accept a number of punitive sanctions, the most severe of which was a twelve-month ban on registering players.

With fantastic photography and exclusive behind-the-scenes shots, this is the remarkable story of the first part of the journey as Ally McCoist led his team to very unfamiliar territory with a thrown-together squad. It's filled with remarkable highs and some crushing lows as well as dramatic developments off the field, which have had a considerable bearing on the road to recovery.

This is the illustrated story of Rangers in the 2012/13 season.

MAY 1937 · IN COMMEMORATION

Presented by
Sir Francis Joseph
KBE. JP. DL.
President of Stoke City.
— F.C. —
to the Members of the
First Division
of the Football League.
GOD SAVE THE KING.

Chapter 1
Turmoil, Turbulence and Takeover

ALLY McCOIST sat at his desk in the match-day manager's office at Ibrox late on Friday, 27 July 2012, frustrated, exasperated and downright angry. With less than forty-eight hours until the first match of the season was due to take place at Glebe Park in Brechin, Rangers had still not been issued with a licence from the Scottish Football Association that would allow them to play football. Looking back, it seems laughable that such a situation should exist, but it was indicative of the shambolic set of circumstances Rangers found themselves in – mostly all as a result of the disastrous tenure of the former owner, Craig Whyte.

McCoist was waiting for confirmation of an agreement being reached between the three football authorities – the SFA, the Scottish Premier League and the Scottish Football League – and the new owners of Rangers, Sevco Scotland, who later became The Rangers Football Club plc. In terms of agreements, it was more Vito Corleone than Entente Cordiale. Rangers' prize money from the previous season's SPL competition, £1.3 million, was withheld. A twelve-month player registration embargo – which was proven at the Court of Session to be unlawful – was foisted upon Rangers and the SPL were free to exploit Rangers' TV rights. At one stage Rangers were even being asked to accept the stripping of five SPL titles and four Scottish Cups won during the period that the club had operated Employee Benefit Trust schemes, even though it had not been proved if they had broken any rules. The fact that it was subsequently decreed by one of Scotland's leading law lords that they had not gained an advantage makes this action all the more abhorrent. Thankfully, these incredible sanctions were fiercely resisted, but reluctantly the club agreed to the rest, reconciling that they could not gamble on the SFA either suspending the club for a year or worse.

McCoist said that night, "Forty-eight hours from now we are supposed to start the season with a game at Brechin, and as I sit here today, I don't know exactly what our status in the game is, where our players that we have should be registered and what the future holds for us going into next week.

"It's a ludicrous situation. No one is denying that Rangers were badly mismanaged for ten months, nor are we disputing that we should be punished for that. We have been. We accept that punishment and want to start putting the past behind us and move forward. But that is not being allowed to happen, and I have to ask myself why.

David Whitehouse, senior partner at Duff & Phelps, and Charles Green at the Murray Park press conference on 13 May 2012 when the sale of Rangers was confirmed.

Charles Green looked on from the meagre directors' seating at Glebe Park, Brechin, with Director of Finance Brian Stockbridge and Head of Football Administration Andrew Dickson.

"In recent days I have been in a number of meetings with Stewart Regan, Rod Petrie and other senior SFA figures, and despair at the lack of leadership shown. In my years in professional football, I have not always agreed with everything the SFA did or said, but no matter what you thought of their decisions, there was no doubt they ran the game firmly and robustly. I can only imagine Ernie Walker looking down on us now and shaking his head in disbelief at the sad state of affairs and the way they have been mishandled.

"As for the SPL, they seem determined to pursue as hostile an agenda as possible towards Rangers. They kicked us out of the SPL – which was their right, and we acknowledge that – but that doesn't seem enough for Neil Doncaster and some of his

board. Not only are they withholding our SPL prize money for last season, they won't tell us how much it is but we reckon it to be about £1.3 million. And having said they don't want us, they do want a bigger share of the TV money that our presence will bring to the SFL and its clubs. Never mind sporting integrity, where is the moral integrity there?

"And there is no line to be drawn in the sand. Rangers have not been punished enough in their eyes, and along with one or two people who have a vested interest within SPL clubs, our right to past titles will be challenged. They want what we and our fans bring, yet seem determined to strip us of every bit of our dignity. It has to stop.

"Sadly, only one Scottish football body has offered us any help or assistance, the SFL, and

I would like to thank David Longmuir, Jim Ballantyne and twenty-nine of their thirty member clubs for inviting us into the SFL. We are grateful for the opportunity. We are looking forward to the challenges ahead, making new friends in the months ahead and having a positive impact on the SFL.

"It is now over five months since Rangers went into administration. It is time to start playing football again, and I am not alone in thinking this."

It was around 9pm that the licence was finally granted and the lateness of the hour meant that Andy Little, who had just signed a new deal with the club, had to be named as a trialist for the Ramsdens Cup first-round tie

at Brechin due to registration protocols. Ian Black, who had signed a three-year contract, did manage to be registered, and he was in the starting line-up too.

And so with no proper pre-season matches under their belts, a thrown-together Rangers squad travelled to the north-east of Scotland to play a game of football, which was something some fans feared may not have happened at all given the bedlam of the previous six months.

Let's rewind further, to 6 May 2011 to be precise, when Craig Whyte completed the purchase of Rangers from Sir David Murray despite opposition from the Independent Board of Rangers, namely Alastair Johnston, Martin Bain, John Greig, John McClelland and Donald McIntyre, and promised to wipe out the £18 million debt owed to Lloyds Bank. He had also taken on the potential liability of a £49 million bill to HMRC for the operation of the EBT schemes, something that the Murray Group, who had operated the schemes, had stoutly proclaimed as not being liable for tax. They were right, but at the wrong time. It was not until 20 November 2012 that the First Tier Tax Tribunal ruled that the majority of the EBT payments were non-contractual and therefore not liable for tax.

Whyte had also promised to invest in the team and the stadium, with a fantasy figure of £25 million bandied about. Instead he wielded the axe on the old board. Johnston and Paul Murray, who was also a vocal sceptic, were removed from the board on 24 May, and both Bain and McIntyre were suspended and never returned to the club and, indeed, raised court actions for unfair dismissal. McIntyre settled on an undisclosed fee in December 2011, and then Bain dropped his action in March 2012 after the payment of costs.

Prophetically, Johnston said at the time, "I will say this. To the 26,000 shareholders and the hundreds of thousands who love the club: be vigilant. Exert pressure on Mr Whyte to support the club financially as he has publicly committed to do. I urge Rangers fans to wield that influence and express that vigilance to ensure he walks the walk and doesn't just talk the talk."

McClelland and Greatest Ranger Greig announced their resignations from the board in October 2011, feeling ostracised from the decision-making process, and that only fuelled more rumour and conjecture.

There had been persistent press reporting that all was not well financially at Rangers under the tenure of Whyte. Indeed, it had been claimed as early as August 2011 that Whyte had paid off the debt to Lloyds with the club's own money by selling future season tickets to Ticketus. He vehemently denied these claims, but it was later revealed that he had, in fact, done exactly that. Whyte had not invested a penny of his own money and had used Rangers' money as part of the transaction to buy Rangers. Incredibly, however, it was also proved that he had concluded this deal with Ticketus before he had completed the purchase with Sir David Murray.

There was worse to come – much worse. Unbeknown to everyone, he had not paid PAYE tax or VAT to HMRC since taking over in May 2011. It seems incredible that HMRC allowed this situation to continue until February of 2012. If an average person is a day late with a tax payment, action is usually taken immediately. Whyte managed to get to the Court of Session before HMRC did and put the club into administration on 14 February, with Duff & Phelps appointed as the administrators. The

Top: Ian Black joined Rangers on a three-year deal on 28 July 2012, having starred for Hearts in the previous season's Scottish Cup Final crushing of Hibs.

Bottom: Chris Hegarty was the first Rangers player to sign a new deal in the summer of 2012 and subsequently a new two-year deal on February 2013.

bill for the non-payment of PAYE and VAT came to £9 million. Rangers fans around the world were shocked and stunned by what had happened and feared for the future, with good reason. Paul Murray rather succinctly summed up Whyte's actions in this way: "It's like someone coming into your house, stealing all of your possessions, and then you are held responsible."

The weeks that followed were horrendous as Duff & Phelps set up camp at Ibrox and pored over the financial mess that was threatening to put the club out of existence. Dramatic measures had to be taken. One million pounds per month had to be saved, and so after protracted negotiations, the players agreed to pay cuts ranging from 75 per cent to 25 per cent for a three-month period, which avoided considerable redundancies among the playing staff.

The fight for Rangers' survival became increasingly serious, but instead of compassionately offering assistance in their time of need, the football authorities went after Rangers with what appeared to be great vigour. The SFA launched an independent inquiry into Rangers and then issued notices of complaint over five breaches of rules to the club and two breaches to Whyte personally. The conclusion of this inquiry was that Rangers should be punished with a twelve-month registration embargo and Whyte banned for life. Despite the fact that it was Whyte who was singularly culpable for the carnage, Rangers as an entity were held responsible for his actions.

In the face of adversity the fans responded incredibly. They virtually sold out every home

Above: The Rangers squad was ravaged when pre-season started on 28 June 2012 with only six recognised first-team players reporting for duty.

Below: The cramped dressing room at Glebe Park, Brechin, laid out neatly by kit controller Jimmy Bell.

match, even though the SPL competition was rendered redundant after Rangers were hit with a ten-point penalty for going into administration. The Rangers Fans Fighting Fund was launched and money poured in from around the globe, which was used tangibly while the administrators sought to find a new owner. Nearly 50,000 watched the Rangers Legends take on AC Milan Glorie on 30 March, raising vital funds for a club in vital need.

The fans' heads were spinning with news of bids from the Blue Knights, a consortium of like-minded individuals headed by Paul Murray and Douglas Park; an American businessman named Bill Miller; Sale Sharks owner Brian Kennedy; and even a Singaporean consortium led by Bill Ng. Duff & Phelps announced Miller, a man who had made his fortune in the tow-truck business, as preferred bidder on 3 May, but within five days he had withdrawn. Then on 13 May – on the morning of the final game of the season – the administrators announced they had signed a binding contract to sell the club to a consortium led by the former

Fans made their feelings known as the football authorities debated Rangers' future in the summer of 2012.

Sheffield United chief executive Charles Green. Green gave a vibrant and colourful press conference at Murray Park on his plans for the club and attended the final match at Perth, where Rangers defeated St Johnstone 4–0.

The Yorkshireman's preferred exit from administration was through a Company Voluntary Agreement, whereby 75 per cent of creditors agree to a package put together by the administrators, but he had also agreed to a sale and purchase agreement and the formation of the 'newco' in the event of the CVA failing. This was viewed as unlikely, as HMRC – as major creditors – had apparently been receptive to the CVA. The bombshell dropped, however, on 12 June when HRMC rejected it and the existing company that owned Rangers was facing liquidation. And so Charles Green and his consortium bought the assets and history of Rangers for £5.5 million under the Sevco Ltd vehicle, which subsequently became The Rangers Football Club Ltd.

Green said, "What we couldn't afford, and what Rangers couldn't afford, was to have a hiatus and then lose time. As unbelievable as it was, and at such a late hour, when HMRC blocked the CVA the structure was in place to continue with the newco option. That said, it was a huge blow and it changed everything dramatically. Whilst corporately we didn't lose any time, we then had to battle with the football authorities to get membership of the FA and to be a member of some league – whichever league that may be. The time that took and the indecision of the SPL clubs meant that valuable weeks were going by without decisions being made and all of that to my mind cast a big shadow over Scottish football."

The other major problem was that leading players invoked what they felt was their right and walked out on their contracts, specifically Steven Naismith, Steven Whittaker, Kyle Lafferty, Allan McGregor, Jamie Ness and Sone Aluko. Steven Davis, John Fleck and Rhys McCabe also left, but compensation

Colin McLaughlin (right) of Ramsdens picked Rangers (ball 8) out of the bag to play Falkirk away in the second round of the Ramsdens Cup. SPL Chief Executive David Longmuir and Gordon Smith, director of football under Craig Whyte, were also involved in the draw.

SPL Chief Executive Neil Doncaster revealed the decision to keep Rangers out of the SPL on 4 July 2012.

Ally McCoist coming off the team bus at the first match of the 2012/13 season – the Ramsdens Cup tie at Brechin on 29 July – with video analyst Steve Harvey to his right.

SFA coach Ross Mathie pulled Rangers out of the hat at the League Cup draw on 20 July, while First Minister Alex Salmond paired them with East Fife. SFL Director of Operations David Thomson looked on.

It was a culture shock for USA national team captain Carlos Bocanegra when he arrived at Brechin on 28 July.

Andy Little was thrilled to sign a three-year deal for Rangers on 28 July but bizarrely had to play as a trialist in the opening game at Brechin.

packages were agreed with Southampton, Coventry City and Sheffield Wednesday respectively. It meant that just thirteen players in total – only six of whom could be considered first-team players – reported for pre-season training on 28 June, and one of these, Chris Hegarty, signed a one-year deal the following day.

It was complete chaos for manager Ally McCoist, and the club's worst fears were realised on 4 July when the SPL clubs refused to allow Rangers into the top flight by blocking the transfer of share from the 'oldco' to the 'newco'. In effect, they booted Rangers out of the top flight but then called on the SFL, to whom Rangers had applied to join, to place Rangers in the First Division for purely financial reasons. The SFL clubs refused to be bullied, and they placed Rangers in Division Three. Never in the history of world football had a top-flight club been plunged down three tiers for forming a 'newco'. Indeed, match-fixing and corruption seem to have been dealt with more leniently, and yet that was the reality for Rangers.

Finally they ran out onto the park at Brechin on 29 July and needed extra time to defeat the Second Division side 2–1, with Lee McCulloch scoring the winning goal. The stadium was packed with supporters, and it was memorable for differing reasons for Graham Clelland and Maggie Tennant, who travelled from Edinburgh to be there on the historic occasion.

Maggie said, "It was the day before Graham's birthday. We took a cake along, so we had a rucksack with us. We went up to the game, had a few beers afterwards, and I had one job and that was to look after the rucksack. We got to the station and suddenly I realised we had left it in the pub. My house keys were in there, so we phoned the bar and they kindly said they would look after it. So we had to go back the next day to collect it."

Graham was not too distressed. He was simply delighted that he had actually seen his team back in action once more. He said, "It was such a relief to see Rangers run out and play at Brechin because only a few days before we didn't know if we would."

For Agnes Douglas from Motherwell it was highly emotional. She said, "My son drove me up along with three other friends, and we were like kids going on an outing. The closer we got to Brechin, the more excited we became. There were tears in

Above: Andy Little scored Rangers' opening goal of the season in the rather fraught Ramsdens Cup tie against Brechin.
Below: Barrie McKay celebrated with Little after his strike at Glebe Park as the delighted fans roared their approval.

my eyes as I walked down to the ground because I honestly thought we wouldn't have been playing. It was really emotional."

McCoist said, "When I look back to last summer, it was madness. We had six players turn up for pre-season training, we couldn't play a pre-season game, we cancelled three tours because we didn't have a licence to play games, and forty-eight hours before we were due to play Brechin in our first game we still didn't have a licence. At the time I didn't realise the level of insanity that was going on around us."

The Journey had started, but it was clear there were going to be bumps along the way. If the Brechin game had taught McCoist and his staff anything it was that it was going to take his thrown-together squad time to get used to their new environment.

The lack of preparation – Rangers had not been allowed to play any proper pre-season matches as a result of being

unlicensed – was clearly a major factor but the players would simply have to find their match fitness as they went along with the expectation that they should sweep all before them.

Rangers had been due to open Le Havre's new stadium on 12 July then come back across the English Channel to face Arsenal and Southampton at St Mary's Stadium on 14 July in the Markus Liebherr Memorial Cup. However, these invitations were withdrawn. Similarly, a three-match tour of Germany where Rangers would have faced Eintracht Braunschweig on 20 July, SV Rodinghausen on 22 July and Armenia Bielefeld on 25 July was also cancelled. Instead, the Light Blues played practice games at Murray Park and it greatly affected their early season form.

Top left: Never camera shy, Charles Green posed for photographers with Malcolm Murray, Brian Stockbridge and Andrew Dickson to his left.

Above left: A packed press conference on 13 July at Hampden following the SFL meeting to consider Rangers' application to join as Chief Executive David Longmuir revealed the Light Blues had been placed in the Third Division.

Top right: Ally McCoist yelled instructions from the bench at Brechin in the first game of the season.

Right: Lee McCulloch, hidden behind Dorin Goian, headed the extra-time winner for Rangers at Brechin.

Welcome to GLEBE PARK home of
BRECHIN CITY FC
Est'd 1906

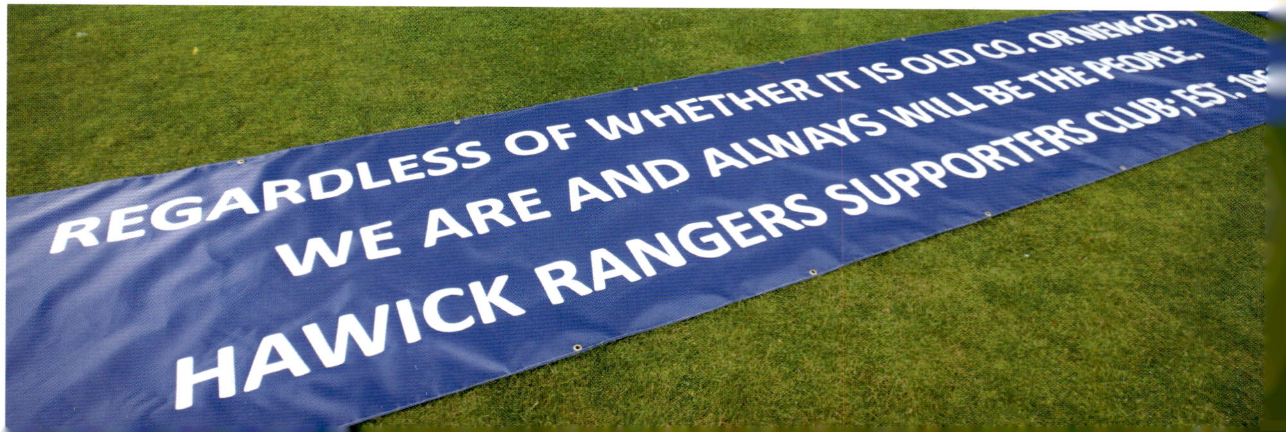

REGARDLESS OF WHETHER IT IS OLD CO. OR NEW CO.,
WE ARE AND ALWAYS WILL BE THE PEOPLE.
HAWICK RANGERS SUPPORTERS CLUB. EST. 19

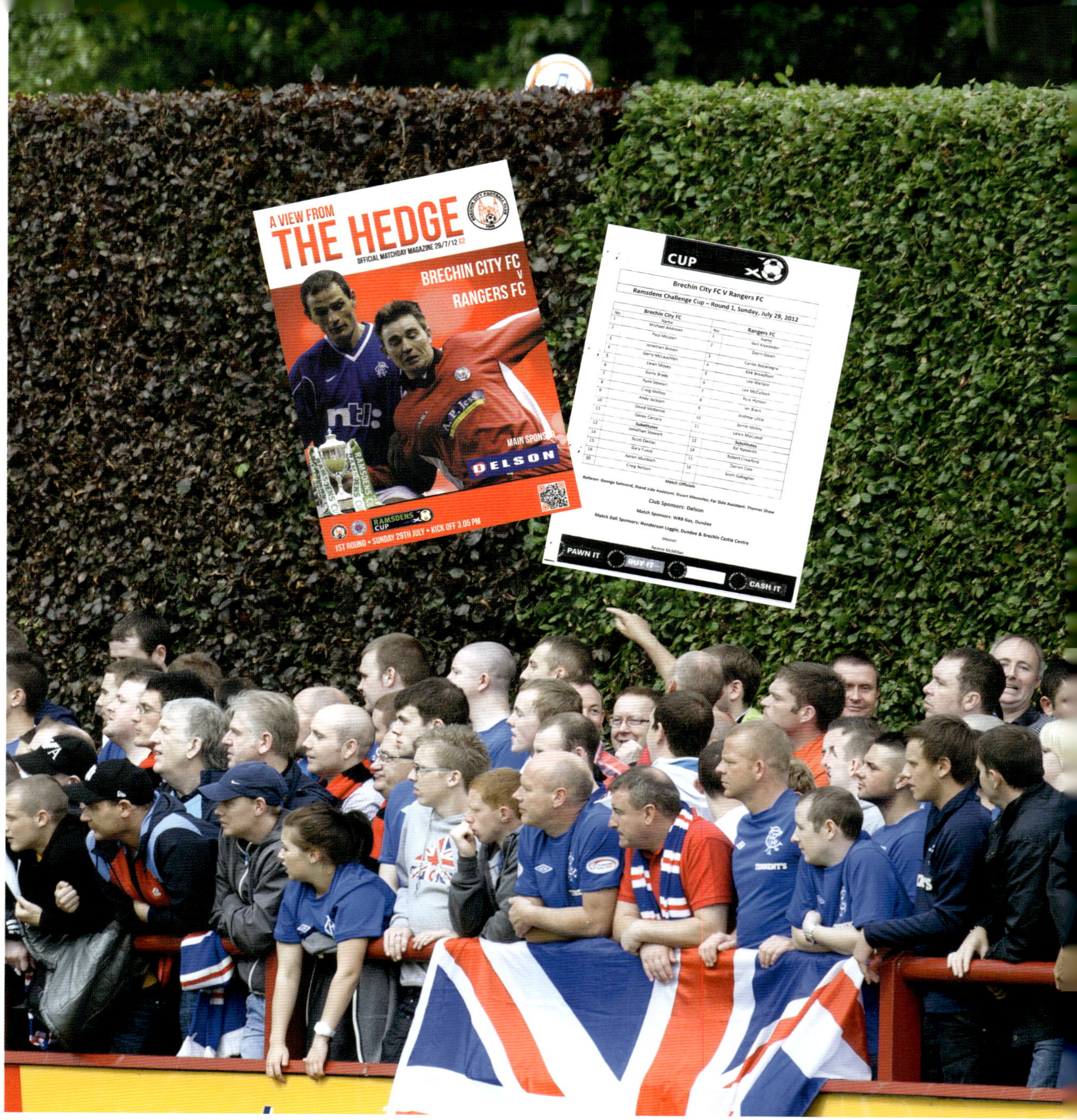

Far top left: It all began for the Rangers supporters in the north-east of Scotland with the Ramsdens Cup tie at Brechin and the mantra was clear: We don't do walking away.

Far middle left: Carlos Bocanegra led Rangers into the 'arena' at Glebe Park, Brechin.

Far bottom left: It was a whole new environment for the Rangers supporters as they sampled life in the lower reaches with the Ramsdens Cup tie at Glebe Park, but the Union Bears were keen to stress that the Light Blues remain world record breakers with 54 Scottish titles.

Top left inset: The match-day programme for the Brechin game on 29 July.

Top right inset: The team line-ups from that historic first match of the season at Glebe Park.

Top left: Football in the smaller stadia of Scotland can have its drawbacks, like the hedge at Glebe Park in Brechin, as the match ball got stuck during the historic Ramsdens Cup tie on 29 July.

Bottom left: Rangers supporters travelled from all corners of the country to be at Brechin for the first match of the 2012/13 campaign, and the lads from Hawick made their feelings known with this banner.

Above: The Rangers supporters were defiant during the dark days of administration.

Right: There was a massive and passionate response from the fans when Rangers faced Kilmarnock on 18 February – just four days after the club plunged into administration.

Top: An astonishing crowd of 49,000 turned out to see the Rangers Legends take on AC Milan Glorie on 30 March 2012.

Far left: Ally McCoist was regularly thrust in front of the cameras during the turbulent summer of 2012.

Left: Rangers legends Walter Smith and Sandy Jardine promoted The Rangers Fans Fighting Fund "1872 Sponsored Walk" at Ibrox on 20 May, which was one of many money-raising schemes in the troubled days of administration.

Chapter 2
Recruitment and Record Breaking

ALLY McCOIST faced a race against time to try to assemble some kind of squad that would not only be capable of winning the SFL 3 Championship, but compete in the domestic cup competitions and entertain the supporters. The twelve-month registration embargo enforced upon Rangers – even though it had been ruled unlawful – was due to kick in on 1 September 2012, so the manager had a month to source new players. It's fair to say he did not secure as many as he would have wanted. Incredibly, he lost twenty-six players between January and August. Davie Weir left at the turn of the year, as did Jordan McMillan and Thomas Kind Bendiksen, while Nikica Jelavic was sold to Everton for £5 million as Craig Whyte desperately tried to bring in cash to stave off administration, but his efforts were in vain.

In the immediate aftermath of the advent of administration, Mervan Celik, who had only arrived in January, left to return to Sweden and Gregg Wylde left for Bolton Wanderers, while Australian midfielder Matt McKay headed to Busan I'Park in South Korea. The exodus in the summer and beyond was remarkable. As previously mentioned, Naismith, Whittaker, McGregor, Lafferty, Aluko and Ness all jumped ship, while compensation was secured for Davis, Fleck and McCabe. Unsung hero Saša Papac had left at the end of the 2011/2012 season to retire from the game, while David Healy, Salim Kerkar, Juan Ortiz, Alejandro Bedoya and goalkeeper Grant Adam were all released.

American stars Maurice Edu and Carlos Bocanegra, Romanian defender Dorin Goian and Kirk Broadfoot had loyally stayed when others fled the parish, but fourth-tier football was never going to be appealing for any of them. By the end of August Edu was sold to Stoke City for around £550,000, while Bocanegra went on loan to Racing Santander in Spain; Goian was loaned to Spezia in Italy and Broadfoot moved to Blackpool on a free transfer.

So it left McCoist with only Neil Alexander, Lee McCulloch and Lee Wallace as regular first-team players from the previous season. The capture of Black from Hearts on a free transfer and the re-signing of Little was crucial, and McCoist followed that by snapping up Dean Shiels, who had been nominated for Player of the Year for his efforts with Kilmarnock. All manner of trialists were brought to Murray Park as the coaching staff frantically tried to make quick judgements while attempting to win games at the same time.

The banner says it all as the fans packed out Ibrox for the opening home game of the season against East Fife when 38,160 turned out to back Rangers.

On 7 August former St Johnstone and Dundee United striker Fran Sandaza arrived, along with Brazilian centre-back Emílson Cribari, who had spent ten seasons in Serie A, as well as former Scotland striker Kevin Kyle, who signed a one-year deal.

That night was an early indication of the phenomenal backing of the Rangers supporters, who turned out in their droves for the first home match of the season, a League Cup first-round tie against East Fife, bossed by former Rangers star Gordon Durie. Remarkably the game was delayed by twenty minutes to allow in a crowd which totalled 38,160, and they were duly rewarded with a convincing 4–0 win, with McCulloch scoring twice, Shiels netting on his debut and Wallace also getting in on the act. And those who were there will never forget the noise that reverberated around the stadium. Colin Kirkwood from Kilwinning said, "I was really concerned that we might not be playing football so when the first game came against East Fife it was great to see so many fans turn out that night.

"When the 'Penny Arcade' tune came on it was electric. It was like an Old Firm game and it was fantastic to be there. After the events of the summer there was a sense of relief too, and everyone was so up for it that night. To see the team come out of the tunnel just lifted everyone."

It was a similarly emotional occasion for Jamal Issa-Lavelle from Glasgow, who said, "The way to talk about Rangers is that it's the longest relationship of your life – although my wife is not too happy about me saying that.

"There were points last summer when I thought there might not be a Rangers and I really was scared. I couldn't contemplate not going to see my team on a Saturday. I thought, 'Am I going to come back to see the team I love?' and I'm so glad that we got there. Men from Scotland and Ulster or wherever are not supposed to cry, but I think lots of us did it the night we played East Fife. We stood there waiting for

the team to come out because the game was delayed to let the crowd in, and the noise when they finally did will stay with me forever. I thought to myself, 'We're still here, after all the turmoil of the summer,' and it made me so proud and so happy."

The attendance at the East Fife game was glaringly indicative that the supporters were ready to back the team in their new environment. However, there is little doubt that some fans were waiting for Ally McCoist to validate the new regime, and when he did ticket sales soared through the roof. He said at the time, "Almost 40,000 fans turned out for the East Fife game last night, over 20,000 season tickets have been sold in just a week and I can't thank the fans enough for their incredible support and loyalty to Rangers.

"The past few months have been extremely difficult for everyone, but this is still Rangers Football Club and the supporters will continue to back us as they have always done. We still play in blue and we are still playing football at Ibrox, so we all have to focus on football again and do all we can to rebuild this great club.

"Now is the time to get right behind Rangers and the best way to do that is to buy season tickets. I encourage all fans to back the club and renew their tickets for Season 2012/13 as we need their support more than ever.

"Filling Ibrox will be vital to Rangers as we begin life in Division Three, and we are delighted to be playing competitive matches again. It is time for everyone with the best interests of Rangers at heart to unite and get behind the club. This is a new chapter for Rangers and we are all looking forward to the challenges ahead. The atmosphere around the stadium has been electric in the past few days and there has been a buzz at the Ticket Centre. This is just the start of the Journey and we will all enjoy it together."

The McCoist seal of approval meant that season ticket sales burst through the 35,000 barrier by the end of the month.

Top right: Ally McCoist was certainly smiling on the touchline despite a horrendous summer, with former Rangers star Gordon Durie in the foreground.

Perhaps in keeping with the bizarre and chaotic nature of the Rangers story, they arrived at Peterhead on 11 August for their historic first match in SFL 3, only to find that they had to wear training shirts. The home strip and the black and blue pin-stripe third kit clashed with Peterhead's blue shirt, while the white second kit was not yet available. It was perhaps an omen of what was to come.

Teenager Barrie McKay gave Rangers the lead, but Jim McInally's side equalised through Rory McAllister, then Scott McLaughlin lashed a left foot shot to give them the lead. Rangers scrambled an equaliser through Andy Little after Kevin Kyle's header was saved.

It was a rude awakening and indicative of the troubles Rangers would have on the road in the early part of the season as they tried to adjust to their new environment. Contrastingly, the fans who went to Balmoor were pleasantly surprised by how welcome they were made in the north-east of Scotland, although the Blue Toon is a bit of a Rangers stronghold.

Jamal Issa-Lavelle was among the throng and he will never forget the trip. He said, "We were walking to the ground and there were people lining the streets and clapping and wishing us all the best. Can you imagine walking through Glasgow and being cheered by the opposition? We had tickets for the home section so we hid our colours, but when Barrie McKay slotted the first goal we were all 'outed', but it was no problem as half of that section were Rangers fans anyway. The locals didn't mind. There was no animosity and they were so welcoming."

And so to Ibrox for the first home league match of the season and the staggering Rangers support reached new heights of excellence. A world record crowd for a fourth-tier regular season league game of 49,118 watched Rangers demolish East Stirlingshire 5–1 and it was a special day for Andy Little, who left with the match ball after grabbing a hat-trick, with McCulloch and Sandaza also on target. There have

Former Scotland striker Kevin Kyle had not played football for eighteen months due to a hip problem, but he was given a one-year deal on 7 August after impressing in training. Sadly injury forced his Ibrox exit before that deal had elapsed.

Spanish striker Fran Sandaza had been a target of McCoist's all summer and he signed a four-year deal on the same day, but it was all to end in tears later in the season.

The pedigree of Brazilian defender Emilson Cribari was impressive after ten years in Italy, including a spell with Lazio where he tasted Champions League action, and he signed a two-year deal on 7 August.

been higher attendances for fourth-tier matches in Brazil – set by Santa Cruz – and in England, but only for play-off matches.

Little said, "I was out of contract and for eleven weeks I didn't really know what I was going to do because things were so up in the air. I knew I had to keep myself fit and I did a lot of training myself when I wasn't attached to the club. I'd go out cycling or for runs around the pitch at my local park. When I did eventually sign, I went straight into the first game against Brechin in the Ramsdens Cup in July, and from there I had to kick on very quickly.

"I wasn't far off the pace when it came to playing, but I wasn't 100 per cent and it was tough, but I couldn't have hoped to make a better start to the season. Getting my first career hat-trick against East Stirlingshire was the high point, although it took me a moment after I'd scored my third goal to realise that was the case. It was an unbelievable feeling for me and it was right up there with anything I've done for the club. It was a special achievement for me."

McCoist continued his frantic recruitment drive as young French defender Sébastien Faure was signed on 21 August on a three-year contract, and then Greek full-back Anestis Argyriou was also brought on board four days later on a two-year deal. In between times, the Light Blues headed to Falkirk and "took the scalp" of the First Division side in the Ramsdens Cup. It was a forgettable game, but Andy Little scored an excellent winner and Chris Hegarty made his Rangers debut.

Off the field there was encouraging news too as a major deal was clinched with Sports Direct to bring the retail operation back in-house following a licensing arrangement with JJB. According to Charles Green, the joint venture

with Sports Direct would have a major effect on revenue and also give Rangers a more global reach. He said, "The key is that fans can buy direct. We were in partnership with JJB and things went well. In terms of my view of how Rangers should look after itself in marketing and branding, to have it in-house is very important. I think the financial figures can be very good. I looked at the historic figures when I was doing my due diligence and I think Rangers Retail with a partner like Sports Direct can achieve a great turnover. This will mean huge amounts of money coming in to help develop the club, develop the team and develop the club worldwide."

On the same day, Rangers were drawn at home to Queen of the South in the third round of the Ramsdens Cup, and there was justified optimism that this was a tie they could win. However, there was more travel sickness in SFL 3 as Rangers struggled to hold Berwick Rangers to a 1–1 draw. A contrite Ian Black said, "Speaking on behalf of all the boys, I think we're all actually embarrassed. I think we know ourselves that was up there with the worst games of football any of us have played in. Every one of us needs to think hard and to take a look at ourselves."

It would be a few weeks before Rangers were able to fully handle playing in such an environment, but they finished the month of August on a high by defeating Falkirk again, this time 3–0 and at Ibrox in the second round of the League Cup. Over 26,000 were there to see Lee McCulloch score twice and Andy Little grab his seventh goal of the month, and all eyes looked ahead to the third-round draw and the prospect of a landing an SPL side.

There was a constant stream of trialists going through Murray Park it seemed and German duo Michael Fink and one-time Bayern Munich back-up keeper Rouven Sattelmaier were two that McCoist decided against.

Above: The SFL 3 journey began in earnest on 11 August and one fan made sure that everyone knew who was in town for the game with Peterhead.

Right: In keeping with the bizarre nature of life in the bottom tier, Rangers, led by Carlos Bocanegra, had to wear training tops for their league opener as their home and third kits clashed with Peterhead's strip and the away kit was not ready.

Far right: Barrie McKay wrote his name into the record books by becoming Rangers' first scorer in SFL 3 when he put the Ibrox men ahead in a match which proved to be very uncomfortable.

It wasn't pretty but it was absolutely crucial, as Andy Little saved Rangers' blushes at Balmoor Stadium in Peterhead when he followed up after Kevin Kyle's header had come back off the bar to bundle the ball into the net, despite the best efforts of the Blue Toon defence, in the final moments to snatch a 2–2 draw.

A then world record crowd of 49,118 watched Rangers flatten East Stirlingshire 5–1 in their first home league fixture of the season on 18 August, and it was a day to savour for Andy Little, who showed off his six pack after clinching a hat-trick.

Legendary Rangers manager Walter Smith looked on approvingly as the crowds packed Ibrox for the first home league game, and it wouldn't be long before he was back at Ibrox for real.

Ally McCoist added to his foreign legion when he gave a three-year deal to Olympique Lyonnais graduate Sébastien Faure, with the defender completing formalities on 21 August.

Rangers headed over the border to play a league match in England for the first time in their history when they faced Berwick Rangers on 26 August, but it was a day they wanted to forget.

Above: The extent of the Journey was glaringly apparent when fans who had been at one end of the country in Peterhead on 11 August found themselves in Berwick on 26 August, but while the sun shone the Rangers performance most definitely did not.

Right: Ally McCoist's seventh signing of the summer was Anestis Argyriou, and the Greek defender had a difficult debut at Shielfield Park against Berwick playing in the left-back slot in a match in which Rangers were fortunate to secure a 1–1 draw.

Above: Coincidentally, Rangers faced Falkirk twice in two different Cup competitions in August and beat them both times. It was Andy Little who made the difference at the Falkirk Stadium on 21 August when Rangers won 1–0 in the Ramsdens Cup.

Right and far right: The Bairns were defeated even more convincingly when Rangers met them at Ibrox in the second round of the League Cup on 30 August, running out 3–0 winners, with Lee McCulloch scoring twice, the first being a header he celebrated with Dean Shiels.

Above and top right: Once Ally McCoist had given the call to supporters to back the club season ticket sales went through the roof as fans flocked to the ticket centre, and by the end of August more than 35,000 had been sold.

Middle right: It may have been fourth-tier football for Rangers but these five young fans were determined to Follow Follow. Chris Newlands, Jordan Burns, Adam Storrie, Callum Boyd and Andrew Harvey show off their season tickets.

Bottom right: As if their travels in SFL 3 were not going to be challenging enough, former Ibrox star Trevor Steven was involved in the Scottish Cup draw on 27 August when the Light Blues were paired with Forres Mechanics away from home.

Chapter 3
Cup Highs and Lows

JUST TWENTY-FOUR HOURS after scoring for Hearts in the Europa League at Anfield against Liverpool, David Templeton became Ally McCoist's blue chip summer signing when he completed a deadline day transfer and signed a four-year deal. Yet just eight minutes into his second match for Rangers in the Third Division on 15 September he badly damaged ligaments in his left ankle and did not play again until December. It was a massive frustration for manager Ally McCoist, who had hoped to make a number of signings before the twelve-month registration embargo kicked in and then lost his only deadline capture for two and a half months.

Templeton had served notice of his quality with two excellent goals in a 5–1 defeat of Elgin at Ibrox on 2 September, but on the synthetic surface at Annan he suffered the injury – and that was not McCoist's only problem. Andy Little returned from Northern Ireland's 2–0 defeat to Russia on 7 September with a foot problem which ruled him out for six weeks, and then Fran Sandaza suffered a horrific cheekbone fracture which put him out for three months, to dampen what had otherwise been an incredible night in the League Cup against Motherwell on 26 September.

Injuries are, of course, an inevitable part of football, but McCoist had warned that his squad was short and was clearly a frustrated man when he lost three key players in quick succession. It was bittersweet for Templeton, whose father Henry, a former Ayr United player, had given his son the middle name of 'Cooper' after the late, great Rangers winger Davie. Templeton said, "The start of September was unbelievable for me, really. I had just played at Anfield and scored against Liverpool and then I signed with Rangers. My first game was two days later and to walk out in front of so many people with 'Simply the Best' being played was something really special. My family were obviously delighted and a few of them came to the game.

"It was one of the best days of my life, and I actually felt all right before the kick-off, I was quite relaxed. The manager had said to me to just go out and enjoy it and do what I do best, basically. There were definitely a few butterflies in my stomach when I walked down the tunnel and Elgin actually went ahead after fifteen minutes with a great goal. Thankfully Deano levelled quickly, and I scored to make it 2–1 before the half-hour mark, which was a great feeling. I then scored again after half-time to make it 4–1, so I was really pleased with

David Templeton was always Ally McCoist's top target before the transfer embargo kicked in and he got his man on deadline day – just twenty-four hours after he had scored at Anfield against Liverpool for Hearts.

Grant Campbell

Top: Templeton made his debut for Rangers on 2 September and it could hardly have gone any sweeter as he scored twice in a 5–1 win over Elgin. This is his first goal, a right-foot strike from close range.

Left: David jumped for joy as he celebrated his first Rangers goal with a familiar face waiting to greet him, former Hearts teammate Ian Black.

Above: The ecstasy against Elgin turned to agony in Annan on 15 September when Templeton severely damaged ligaments in his left ankle and was out of action for ten weeks.

both goals, especially the first, and to win 5–1 in the end was brilliant.

"It was the perfect start to my Rangers career, but I then went to Annan and I took a bad one on my ankle and I was out for ten weeks. I think it was one of my first touches of the ball in that game so I was gutted after that, and the boys were disappointed to draw 0–0 down there as well."

The Annan result was another stinker. Rangers just could not seem to produce the level of performance needed on their travels. That said, travelling to the small town in Dumfries and Galloway was fun for the fans. Jamal Issa-Lavelle said, "The father-in-law of a friend of mine lives in Annan and he met me before the game, and I never had to pay for a drink!

"We got to the ground and I couldn't see anything for the first five minutes because I'm only 5ft 6in – including the injury to David Templeton. Then I noticed a few Bears were climbing onto a wall so I managed to join them – even if I needed a punt up. So I was perched up there, hanging onto a fence behind me, and I managed to watch the game and then I turned to my left and there was a blow-up banana. I have followed Rangers all over Europe and never in my days did I think I would be sitting on a wall in Annan next to a banana."

By this point Rangers had a new leader on the field. Following the departure of Carlos Bocanegra to Racing Santander on loan, there really was only one choice for skipper, and it was Lee McCulloch. Unlike others who fled in the summer, McCulloch showed his loyalty and commitment to remain with the club and pledge his future despite the lowly surroundings, and he was genuinely humbled to take the armband.

He promptly celebrated the occasion with two goals in that 5–1 victory over Elgin on 2 September. He said, "It was a day I will remember for a while. The gaffer had told me on the Saturday that he was going to make me the official captain

Top: Ally McCoist conducted some very astute business in the famous Ibrox manager's office on 11 September when rising stars Barrie McKay, Lewis Macleod and Robbie Crawford all committed to the club for five years.

Bottom: Lee Wallace had no hesitation in putting pen to paper on a new five-year deal on 14 September, insisting that the supporters were the main inspiration for his decision. He was one of only a handful of senior players to have committed to the club after the newco transfer.

and I wasn't able to stop smiling. I had a bit of a virus and I didn't feel the best, but after the gaffer told me I was going to be captain there was no way I was going to miss the Elgin game.

"It's one of the proudest moments in my life to be made captain. To lead the team out in front of nearly 50,000 at Ibrox is something you dream about as a kid. It's a dream to play for the club, but to become captain? That's something for the grandkids."

McCulloch and Rangers were in cup action in September in three different competitions, which produced emotions of disappointment, elation and relief. First up it was Queen of the South at Ibrox in the quarter-finals of the Ramsdens Cup on 18 September in what proved to be a controversial night, as the Dumfries men snatched a dramatic last-minute equaliser to force extra-time, and then won the tie 4–3 on penalties.

With the Ibrox connection of Allan Johnston and Sandy Clark in their technical area, it was the assistant manager's son Nicky who gave Queens the lead with a good header, but then Barrie McKay equalised and McCulloch slotted a penalty twenty minutes from time. Kevin Kyle was sent off for an alleged elbowing incident, and then Willie Gibson was dismissed for a second yellow card in the last minute, but Queens found an equaliser in injury-time and it was Clark who set up Gavin Reilly, who looked offside.

Queens prevailed in the shoot-out and went on to win the trophy in what was a quite remarkable season, as they also won the Second Division title by a record points margin. In normal circumstances, if a Rangers side lost at home to Queen of the South there would be hell to pay, but these, of course, were far from normal circumstances.

In stark contrast, McCoist's men produced their best performance of the season when they met Motherwell in the third round of the League Cup on 26 September and stormed

Top left: These hardy souls from Hereford decided to make a weekend of it when Rangers faced Annan Athletic for the first time on 15 September, although the accommodation looks as though it was a bit of a squeeze.

Above: Going to Galabank Stadium in Annan was also going to be an experience in itself, but bizarrely the Rangers supporters were joined by an inflatable banana.

Left: Rangers were still getting used to the rough and tumble of SFL 3 when they travelled to Dumfries-shire, but it looks as though Lee McCulloch was getting the hang of it.

Rangers and Liverpool are two great football clubs with histories of glory and success, but they are also bound by tragedy after sixty-six died at the Ibrox Disaster in 1971 and ninety-six Liverpool fans lost their lives in the Hillsborough Disaster in 1989. A minute's silence for the ninety-six was held at Ibrox ahead of the Ramsdens Cup tie against Queen of the South on 18 September, following the release of the independent report into the events at the FA Cup semi-final with Nottingham Forest.

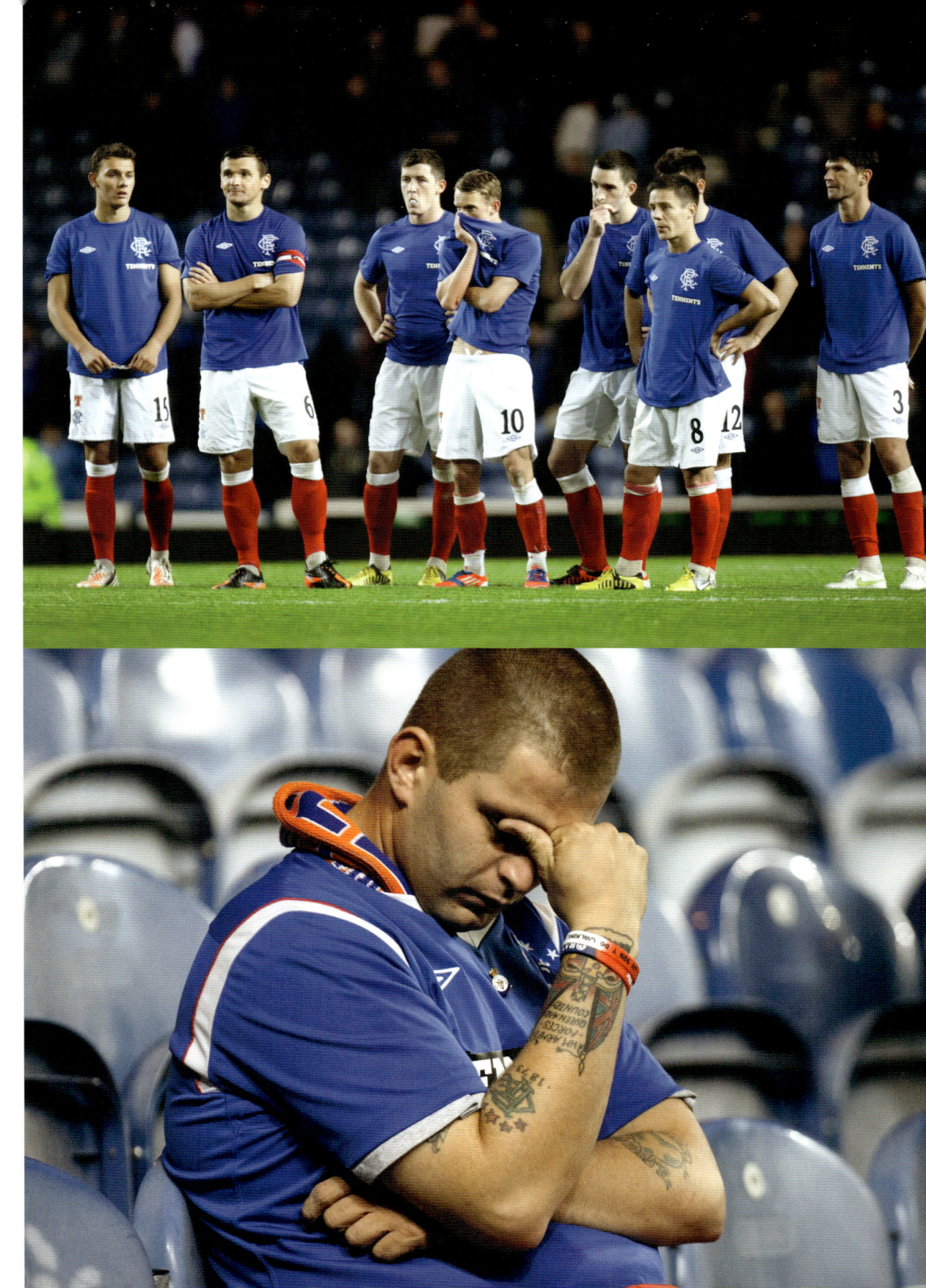

to a superb 2–0 victory in front of just under 30,000 at Ibrox. Dean Shiels set up Lee McCulloch for a classic header, and then the Northern Irishman volleyed in the second goal from Anestis Argyriou's cross to defeat the side that was top of the SPL at the time. The fans revelled in the result as an SPL side had been firmly poked in the eye, and it was a performance that ticked all the right boxes in terms of tempo, passing, desire and finishing. The team never managed to reach those heights again in the campaign. It was perhaps the challenge of playing against a top-flight side that inspired them. While subsequently achieving good results and performances, Rangers never quite reached the standards they set in that Motherwell match.

As if to exacerbate that point, the Light Blues toiled in their next encounter. They had drawn Forres Mechanics of the Highland League in the second round of the Scottish Cup and headed for Mosset Park on 29 September. In the end Kal Naismith's left-foot finish from fourteen yards was all that separated the sides, and there were one or two frightening moments for goalkeeper Neil Alexander as the Highlanders threatened an upset.

In between the Queen of the South and Motherwell matches, Rangers produced another comprehensive win at home in the league when they defeated Montrose 4–1 on 23 September, with the highly impressive Lewis Macleod scoring his first goal for the club, and fellow Youth Academy graduate Robbie Crawford followed suit. It was perhaps written in the stars, as both youngsters signed five-year contracts with Rangers on 11 September, while Barrie McKay also made the same commitment, although the paperwork could not be completed until his eighteenth birthday in January. It was astute business by Ally McCoist, and there was more exciting contractual news on 14 September when Lee Wallace signed a new five-year contract which instantly committed him to the cause of leading Rangers all the way back to the top.

Above: Passion plays a huge part when it comes to following Rangers and one supporter at the Montrose game on 23 September made his feelings known about the players who refused to transfer over to the new company who now run the club.

Right: Ally McCoist hit his landmark fiftieth birthday on 24 September and he was presented with this giant cupcake as a gift at the Montrose match the day before when his team made it a happy birthday weekend with a 4–1 win.

He insisted that the supporters were largely responsible for his decision. He said, "The fans have held us together in a lot of ways. They've been tremendous. They were a major factor in me wanting to sign on. When things weren't going well towards the end of last season, they were still supporting us in their numbers. Even on the back of some poor defeats, they were standing up applauding us and the atmosphere was still great. They've been a huge factor in a number of the boys who have come here signing on as well and it's great.

"It has been a great time since the start of the season. The prospect of going into the Third Division was a bit of a downside at the time, but having now experienced it and having come in to train every day, it has been great and I've been enjoying it.

"The new guys who have come in have brought a real freshness to the squad and improved it, which was good. I was happy to sign the deal. It gives me a bit of long-term security and I'm enjoying the adventure we are going on."

Equally exciting for the supporters was the announcement on 7 September that Cenkos Securities had been recruited to assist with the plan of listing the club on the Stock Market. However, with every silver lining there came a cloud, it seemed. The SPL announced on 10 September that they were setting up a commission, headed by respected judge Lord Nimmo Smith, to investigate alleged breaches of SPL rules over Rangers' usage of Employee Benefit Trusts between 2000 and 2011, which allowed the recipients – mostly players – to avoid paying tax. The very clear threat over these investigations was that if it was agreed that serious breaches took place then the SPL would try to strip Rangers of five Championships – something, of course, they tried to do before any investigation when the five-way negotiations on an SFA licence took place in July.

Top left: You can see what it meant to Dean Shiels to score in the 4–1 win over Montrose when he displayed the type of form that the fans knew he was capable of.

Top centre: Is it a bird? Is it a plane? No, it's Super Lee after powering a header in the Motherwell net to give Rangers the lead in a fantastic League Cup win over the Steelmen on 26 September.

Top right: It was a black night, however, for Spanish striker Fran Sandaza, who suffered terrible facial injuries following a challenge by Motherwell defender Shaun Hutchison which put him out for ten weeks.

Bottom left: The scoreboard at Ibrox tells the story and there is little doubt that the performance against the Lanarkshire side was the best of the season.

Bottom right: McCulloch, who started his career with Motherwell, saluted the fans who lapped up the 2–0 victory against Stuart McCall's side, who were top of the SPL at the time.

Top: Tickets were like gold dust in the Highlands for the historic Scottish Cup meeting with Forres Mechanics in the second round of the Scottish Cup on 29 September.

Bottom: One young fan waved his red and black scarf at Mosset Park. These scarves were sold at the height of the administration traumas to raise much-needed cash for the Fans' Fighting Fund.

The reaction from the club was one of anger. Indeed, Charles Green said that Rangers would not take part in the proceedings and vowed that they would never relinquish any titles. The fact that the commission would exonerate Rangers from gaining any kind of sporting advantage through the use of EBTs five months later clearly validates the club's stance at this time.

On a similarly distasteful note, the BBC were taken to task for the opening sequence to their coverage of the League Cup tie with Motherwell on 26 September. It was an animated montage based on the US TV show *Mad Men*, it depicted a Rangers official, clearly manager Ally McCoist, falling from an office window at Ibrox and smashing a club crest. No apology was forthcoming from the BBC, and Rangers subsequently withdrew all co-operation a month later. As ever, the Journey was proving to be a bumpy ride for everyone connected with the club.

Preparing for the visit of Rangers was always going to be tricky for Forres Mechanics and there was scope for a group of fans to get a free view from outside the boundary wall.

It's not quite a garden party as we know it, but some lucky Rangers fans got to watch the Cup action from a local resident's home, complete with al fresco refreshments.

Everyone wanted to see Rangers in Cup action and they would do anything to catch a glimpse, even if it meant standing on top of a satellite TV truck.

The logistics of Mosset Park meant that there were vantage points for some fans who did not have tickets for the game, although some were clearly more comfortable than others.

Forres Mechanics Football Club

Right: The Rangers management and backroom staff all looked a bit too close to the Mosset Park action for comfort. Indeed, Dr Paul Jackson looked decidedly uncomfortable perched inside the old-fashioned dugout.

Bottom left: Ibrox seemed like a world away when Rangers headed to the Highlands to face Forres and the Light Blues only scraped through winning 1–0.

Bottom right: It was Kal Naismith who scored the only goal of the match against Forres – his first for the club – and there was a feeling of relief more than anything else that the Light Blues had gone through.

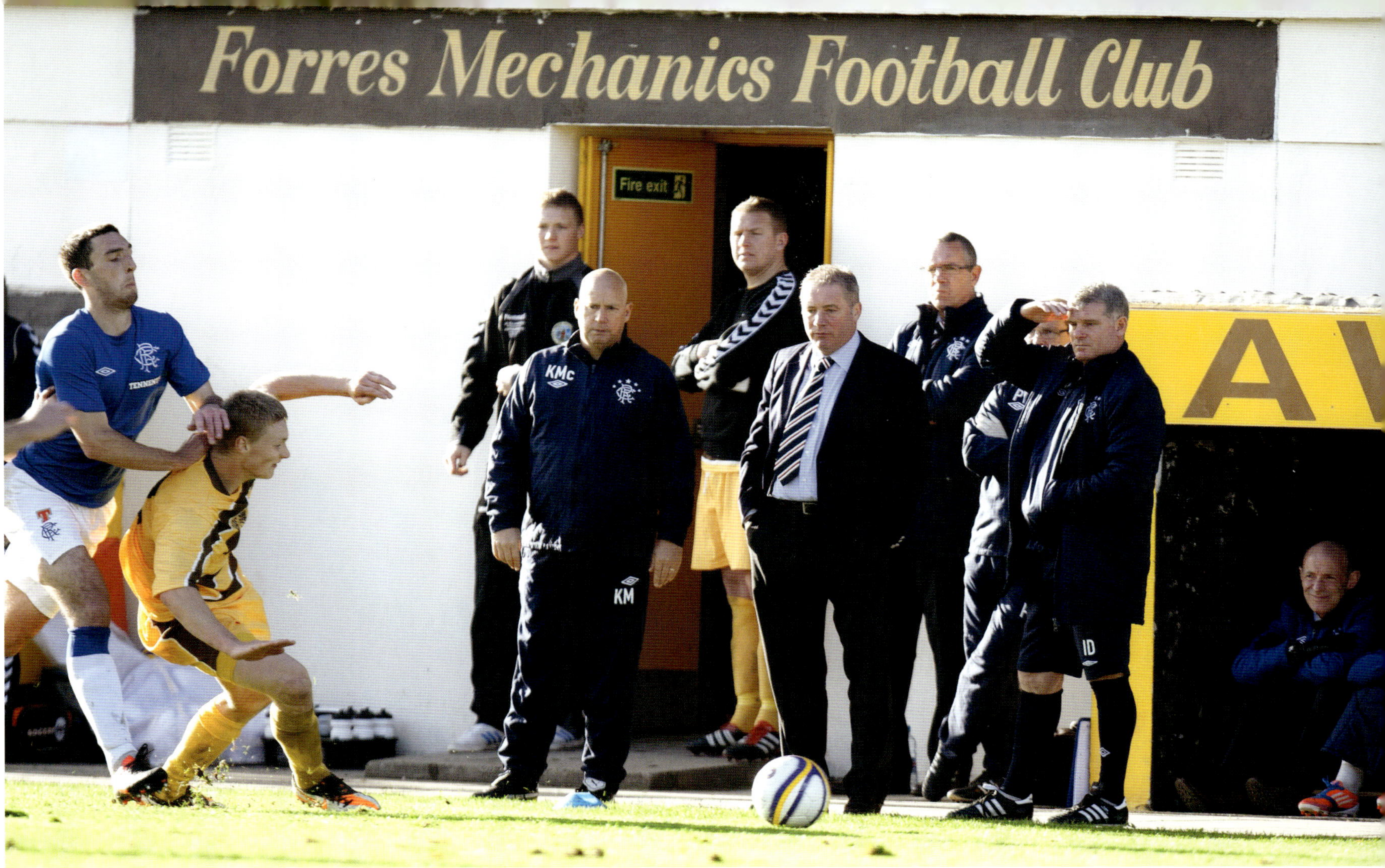

The official team line-up for the 2012/13 season – Back (from left to right): Davie Lavery (masseur), Robbie Crawford, Ross Perry, Kamil Wiktorski, Fran Sandaza, Emilson Cribari, Kevin Kyle, Lee Wallace, Kal Naismith, Kyle Hutton, Steve Walker (physiotherapist), Andy Dunlop (sports scientist). Middle: Gary Sherriff (sports scientist), Jimmy Bell (kit controller), Chris Hegarty, Darren Cole Anestis Argyriou, Sébastien Faure, Neil Alexander, Scott Gallacher, Lee McCulloch, Andy Little, Kane Hemming, Andy Mitchell, Stuart Collie (physiotherapist), Steve Harvey (video analysis). Front: Adam Owen (head of sports science), Pip Yeates (physiotherapist), David Templeton, Dean Shiels, Lewis Macleod, Kenny McDowall (assistant manager), Ally McCoist (manager), Ian Durrant (first team coach), Barrie McKay, Ian Black, Francesco Stella, Jim Stewart (goalkeeping coach), Dr Paul Jackson.

Chapter 4
Share of the Spoils

IT WAS perhaps ironic yet indicative of the rollercoaster ride that Rangers were on that the club should announce its plans to list on the AIM market of the London Stock Exchange just days after a quite dismal result on the field. In normal circumstances a 1–0 defeat away to Stirling Albion, which occurred on 6 October, would rank as arguably the worst result in the club's history. However, these were not normal circumstances by any means. Indeed, five days later Charles Green, Ally McCoist and finance director Brian Stockbridge were in the UK capital to formally announce their intention to raise up to £20 million through an Initial Public Offering – IPO. The sceptics, of course, disparagingly dismissed this idea as fanciful at best – but they did not bank on the pulling power of Rangers and, giving credit where it is due, the sales skills of Green.

Manager McCoist was in no doubt that it was a very important day – especially as the IPO would allow thousands of fans to make their own investment in the club. It was a day he probably did not envisage when he was caught in the maelstrom of administration just a few months earlier. He said at the time, "It's another massive step in the process. We've come a long way in a short space of time and we've still a long way to go, but today is another step in the right direction.

"It's a big step for the club in the respect we can hopefully raise income for it to go forward, which will be used to benefit the club and the supporters.

"I'm absolutely thrilled the supporters can invest. It gives them the opportunity to invest in their club. That is very, very important – I know how important that is to them to do that.

"One of the major positives will be that the income raised will be going back into the club, and being a supporter myself, I know how important it is to invest in the club. We've all had our traditions throughout the 140 years of Rangers so far. Families have supported the club throughout in that time and they've taken a keen interest in its future. Of paramount importance is that the future of the club cannot be put in jeopardy again. Looking back, I don't think some people realise how close we might have been to extinction. That would have affected hundreds of thousands of people. That's how important the club is to so many of us. That, it goes without saying, must not be allowed to happen again.

"We must be strong and solid and the supporters must see that and have faith in it because everybody involved with the club had a very traumatic time this year."

Lee McCulloch couldn't hide his bitter disappointment as he left the field at Forthbank on 6 October after Rangers had suffered the shock 1–0 defeat to Stirling Albion.

Press Association

It was painful for Ally McCoist to look as the final whistle sounded at Forthbank following the 1–0 win for Stirling Albion, which was joyously celebrated by Graham Weir.

Less than a week later Green was able to report that over 8,000 fans had already registered for shares and he had yet to seek commitments from institutional investors, which would provide the lion's share of the capital investment. There was hard work ahead in that regard, but the early indications were that the share issue was on course to buck the trend of investment in football clubs.

There were changes to the corporate structure of the club too when Green's close colleague Imran Ahmad was appointed Commercial Director, charged with driving new business, while one of the founder investors, Craig Mather, was made Director of Sports Development, with the job of reviewing the overall organisational structure and assuming financial responsibilities for Murray Park. Few would have predicted then that before the end of the season both Green and Ahmad would be gone and Mather would be the new captain of the ship.

Green seemed to have the supporters eating out of his hand at this point, but his propensity for being outspoken led to an own-goal when he gave an interview to *The Sun* and told them he had received death threats during the takeover process. He argued that he was merely trying to illustrate how far everyone had come together since these days, but it was clearly a mistake. He would make more and in the end his brashness would cost him.

On the field, as previously mentioned, Rangers made a terrible start to the month with the defeat at Forthbank on 6 October against the side ranked bottom of the pile in Scottish football. Brian Allison's goal in eight minutes was enough to achieve a famous victory for Albion who, incredibly, achieved the massive upset without the guidance of their manager Greig McDonald. He missed the greatest victory in Albion's sixty-seven-year history because he was getting married to fiancée Jennifer at Solsgirth House, near Dollar.

Press Association

Grant Campbell

Top right: On 11 October Charles Green, Brian Stockbridge and Ally McCoist held a press conference at the London Stock Exchange to announce their intention to list Rangers on the AIM market.

Middle right: Legendary Rangers goalkeeper Bobby Brown got together with the modern No.1 Neil Alexander at the quarter-final draw for the League Cup on 4 October when Rangers were paired with Inverness. Brown, who celebrated his ninetieth birthday on 19 March 2013, played and won the first ever League Cup Final in 1946/47 and was part of the first ever Rangers Treble team in 1948/49.

Bottom right: Another Rangers great, Derek Johnstone, was on hand to help out at the Scottish Cup third-round draw on 1 October when the Light Blues were drawn at home to face Alloa.

McCoist was honest with his assessment. He said, "I've had painful defeats before, but that's certainly very painful. As disappointed as I am – and I am bitterly disappointed – it's not the end of the world because we get the sleeves rolled up and come out of it the other side. The players are disappointed too, as they should be, but we will bounce back from this, no doubt.

"I felt we created numerous chances but didn't take them. When we don't take our chances we run the risk of being punished and that's what happened. We had some fantastic chances in the second half as well, but when you don't take them you get punished and we didn't do it in either half.

"It's one thing saying that we need to come to these grounds, roll up our sleeves and go into battle with them, but we can all talk a good game, it's time for action."

Due to the international break, Rangers had to wait two weeks to get the Stirling shock out of their system, but they did just that on another special Ibrox day as Rangers defeated Queen's Park 2–0 on 20 October and smashed their own attendance record for a fourth-tier league match when 49,463 watched the original Glasgow derby.

Lee McCulloch scored both goals that day, which took his remarkable tally to twelve goals in thirteen matches, and he was also on the score sheet the following weekend when Rangers finally banished the away day blues.

There is little doubt that the 2–0 win over Clyde at Broadwood on 28 October was a pivotal moment in the season, as it sparked a succession of victories on the road which would ultimately drive Rangers to the title with some ease. Ulsterman Dean Shiels gave Rangers a spectacular lead with a fantastic looping shot, and after a few missed opportunities, McCulloch made sure of the win. Rangers were top of the table and there was no looking back.

McCulloch said, "I remember the game up in Stirling well. It was our first defeat of the season and it was a hot day, the pitch also wasn't the best, although I'm not trying to make excuses. But after that game I think reality kicked in that it was not going to be the fairy-tale season that maybe fans, players and everybody thought it might be.

"We knew we had to step up if we were going to win the title and that was a real low point coming into training following that result. We then had our match against Queen's Park two weeks later, the Glasgow derby, and there had to be a reaction. We couldn't crumble and had to keep going. I was down myself but as captain I knew I had to snap out of that quickly and help our younger ones, especially as we knew Queen's were a good side.

"In the first half we started pretty well then dipped, and at half-time there were a few arguments and I was involved in them. But something had to change there and then and the boys went out and we won comfortably.

"That game meant loads to me as big Davie Weir was in the directors' box and I managed to get two goals and gave him a wave. I remember the atmosphere and the stadium was full, the match-day programme also looked great with the old-style cover. There was something a bit different about that afternoon and after losing to Stirling, there was no way we could have lost that game.

"Thankfully we then went on to beat Clyde to get our first away victory of the campaign on their 3G pitch. I had never played on that kind of surface before, but Deano scored a

Far left: Kevin Kyle reckons it was written in the stars that he should play for Rangers after he found out he was loosely related to the famous winger of the 1920s and 1930s, Alan Morton, whose portrait hangs at the top of the marble staircase. Kevin's great-grandfather was Alan Morton's cousin.

Top left: Ian Black helped launch a special limited edition pink shirt in support of the Rangers Charity Foundation in conjunction with Sports Direct on 18 October. Only 5,000 shirts were made and over £60,000 was raised for the Foundation.

Above: Rangers were given a specially commissioned plate by Forres Mechanics to mark the Scottish Cup tie between the sides at Mosset Park in September and it was placed in the Trophy Room in October. It depicts twenty-two sheep in Forres and Rangers strips playing each other at football with the Moray town's backdrop, including the iconic Nelson Tower, in the background.

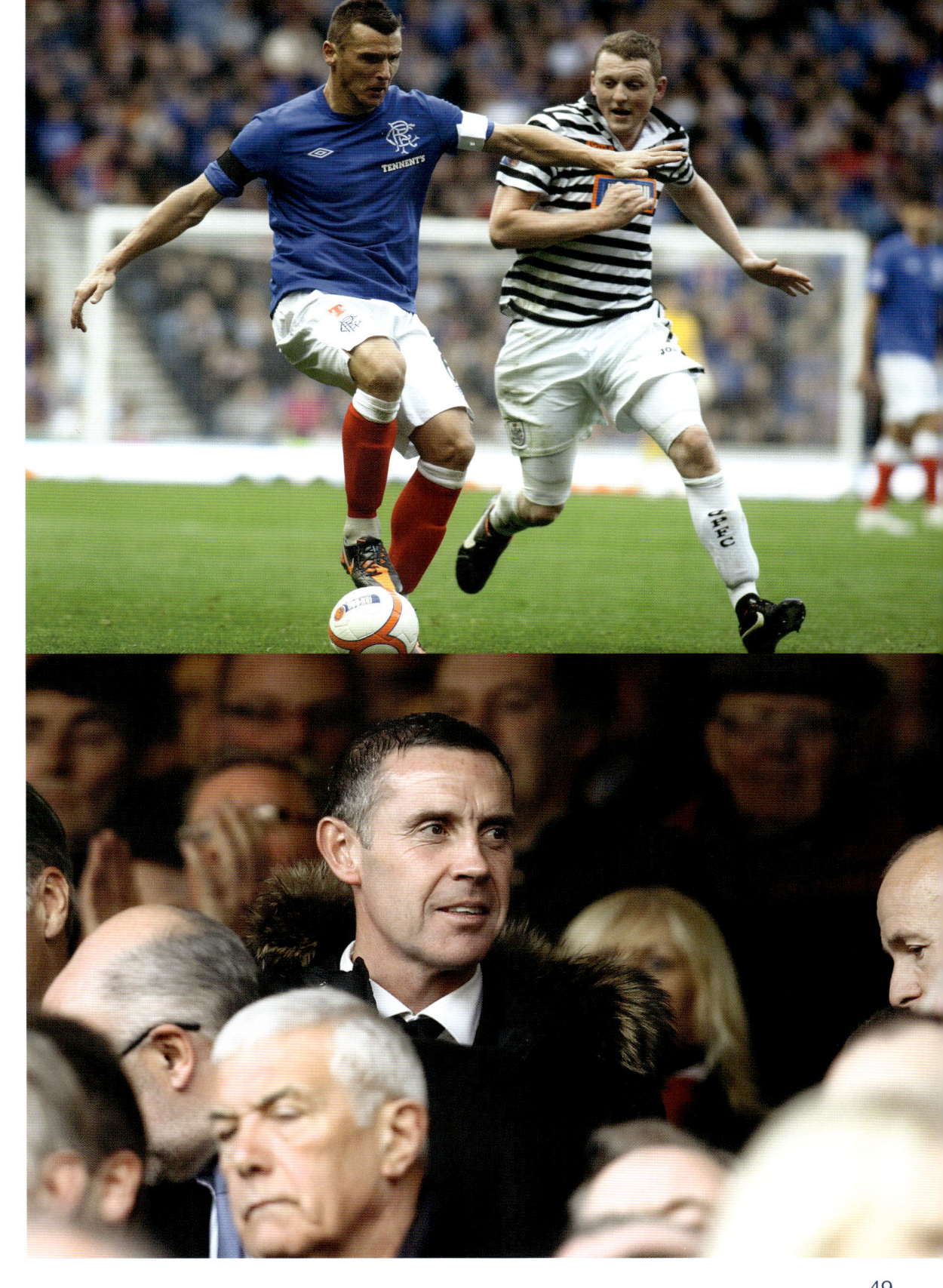

brilliant goal right into the top corner and there was a lot more confidence in our performance.

"We dominated, and I remember in the second half I missed an absolute sitter and thought I was going to be subbed. Thankfully I managed to score a tap-in after good play from Blackie. There is no doubt the result at Broadwood gave us the chance to kick on in the league."

Unfortunately, the month finished disappointingly for Rangers when they were rather unceremoniously dumped out of the League Cup by Inverness Caledonian Thistle on 31 October, when the hopes and dreams of many fans where shattered. It may have been a romantic notion, but having beaten Motherwell so convincingly in the previous round, many hoped that Rangers could replicate that form and move into the semi-finals. The fans were starting to daydream that a Rangers team in the Third Division could go on to lift the trophy, but Inverness won convincingly in the end, producing a 3–0 victory at Ibrox.

There was an argument that failing to progress was a blessing in disguise, because it lengthened the odds of facing Celtic and, in all honesty, this Rangers team was not ready for that challenge.

As if to add insult to injury it was Murray Park graduate Andy Shinnie who was the best player on the park. He opened the scoring and was brought down for a penalty, which was converted by his brother Graeme, with Gary Warren scoring in between times.

Perhaps more galling for those Rangers fans left in the stadium at the end was the over-reaction of manager Terry Butcher, who danced across the Ibrox pitch towards the small band of Caley fans, punching the air with both fists as if he had just won the Cup. Many fans felt this was not an appropriate way to behave given he had captained the club for four years – albeit nearly twenty-five years earlier – and is revered by the supporters as an iconic figure.

McCoist was once again candid with his views. He said, "The second half was very disappointing. I thought the individual errors that created the three goals were very disappointing. In the second half Inverness were better than us and deserve to be in the semis more than we do.

"It was an opportunity for us to play against an SPL team, which we did do against Motherwell, but the intensity in

Top right: Sandy Jardine was thrilled to take possession of the famous No.6 shirt worn by Jim Baxter in Scotland's memorable 3–2 victory over England at Wembley in 1967 when the then World Champions were humiliated by the Scots, who were bossed by Bobby Brown. Jimmy McGarrity had been given the shirt by former Chelsea midfielder Alan Hudson who, in turn, had received it from Alan Ball, who swapped shirts with Baxter after the game.

Bottom right: Multi-million selling singer-songwriter Amy MacDonald shows her true colours in this exclusive shot taken in October. Amy is proud to be a lifelong Rangers supporter and wrote a song called 'The Green and the Blue' which reflects the rivalry in Glasgow.

which we played was miles short of what we showed against Motherwell. We got what we deserved in the second half and so did Inverness.

"It probably is a reminder of how far we have to travel, but I'm extremely aware of how far we have to travel. There is a thin line, because it is very difficult in the sense that I will never make excuses for the second-half performance. The league remains our top priority and the cups are a bonus."

McCoist's gloom would be washed away within a matter of days with the welcome return of a loyal friend and mentor.

Above: Ally McCoist was at Edinburgh Castle as the famous One O'Clock Gun was fired to confirm ABF The Soldiers' Charity as the Rangers Charity Foundation's new National Charity Partner for season 2012/13. The Soldiers' Charity, the Army's national charity, has been working with soldiers and veterans from every conflict since World War II by giving practical support to the brave men and women who serve in the British Army.

Top right: A select group of Rangers fans were lucky enough to attend the 1964 Treble Legends Lunch on 26 October, where they were regaled with great tales from Jim Forrest, Ralph Brand and Davie Wilson, with celebrity Bluenose Andy Cameron posing the questions.

Top far right: Ralph Brand was easily one of the best goal-scorers Rangers ever had, with an incredible strike rate of 206 goals in 317 games when the Light Blues dominated the early 1960s.

Bottom right: Davie Wilson was equally prolific, even though he played on the left wing and on the day he did play through the centre – 17 March 1962 – he smashed a double hat-trick against Falkirk and remains the last Rangers player to score six times in a competitive match.

Bottom far right: Of course Rangers needed a good back line in the 1960s, and Billy Ritchie was a reliable goalkeeper. Sandy Jardine was delighted to catch up with him at the lunch.

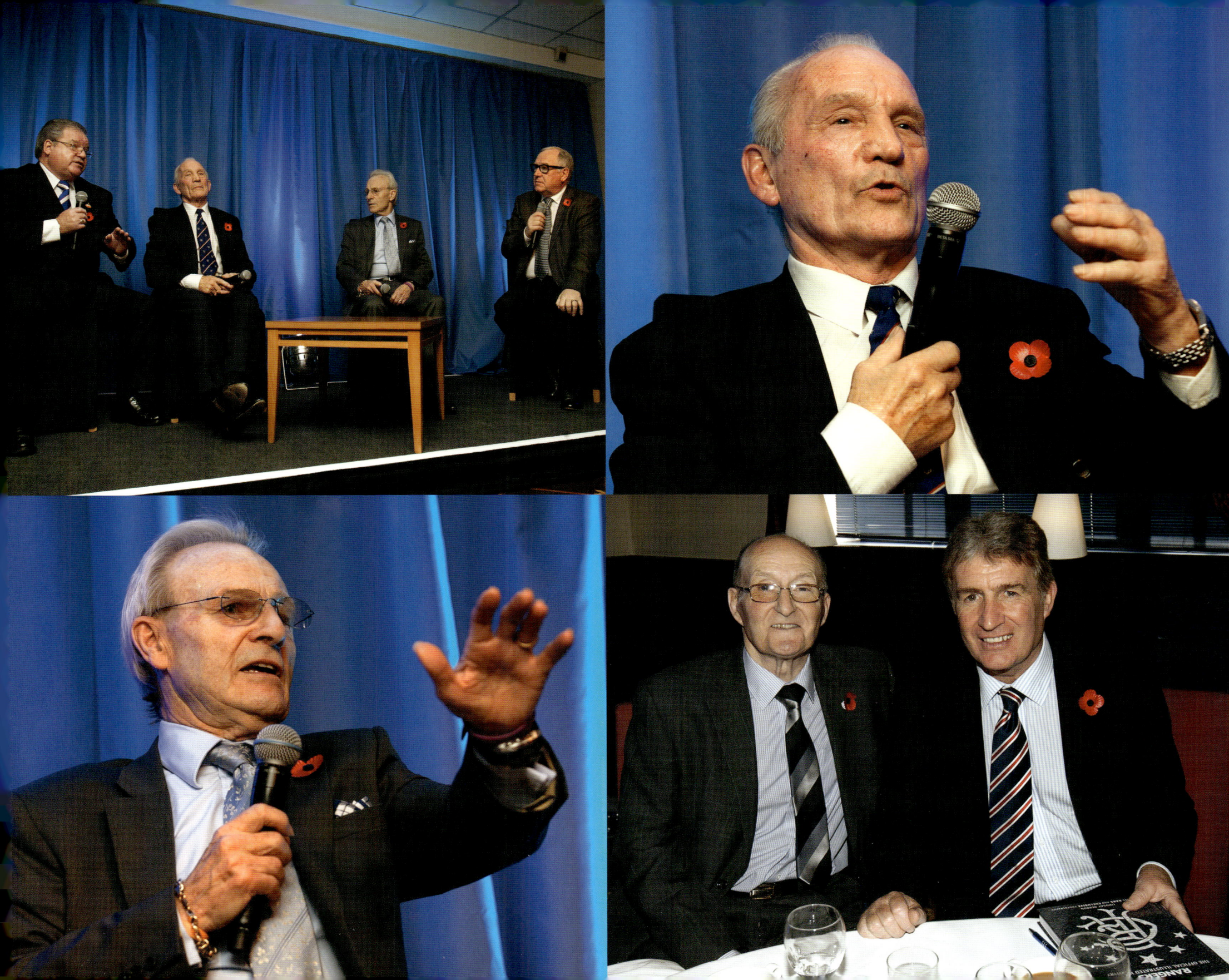

Top left: These Rangers fans decided to add their own nationalistic touch to the Blue Man Group theme as they got into the party mood for the Halloween meeting with Inverness at Ibrox which, unfortunately, turned into a bit of a nightmare.

Top middle: These girls went down the Minnie Mouse route as they got dressed up for the occasion and their costumes certainly went down well with the bloke next to them!

Top right: There were some witches at Ibrox on 31 October too, but sadly they couldn't work their magic to secure a Rangers win as the Highlanders ran out 3–0 winners.

Left: Lee Wallace battled with ICT's Aaron Doran during the League Cup quarter-final which ended in such huge disappointment for the players and the fans.

Chapter 5
Return of a Legend

IT IS undoubtedly fair to say that there were many Rangers men who were sceptical about the motives of Charles Green when he burst onto the scene to take control of Rangers in May 2012. One such sceptic who carries considerably more weight than most was Walter Smith. Indeed, such were his concerns that he happily fronted a rival consortium, backed by Jim McColl and Douglas Park, in an attempt to buy the club back from Green and his group. His timing was not great. Green had just completed the purchase of the club and formed the newco – which would become The Rangers Football Club Ltd – following the collapse of the CVA at the hands of HMRC.

Smith said in a statement at the time, "I can confirm that following talks over the last few weeks I am leading a new bid for Rangers Football Club. I have been assisted by Jim McColl, Douglas Park and other prominent Scottish businessmen with a shared objective – that Rangers Football Club should be in the hands of Rangers people who will stabilise the club and protect it from future situations like we find ourselves in today.

"With this in mind, representatives have, on behalf of my group, made representations to BDO, Duff & Phelps and indeed Charles Green, notifying them of our willingness to offer on the 'newco' basis on which Mr Green is proceeding.

"We would call on Mr Green to step aside and allow us to proceed with our deal, which is in the best interests of the creditors, the employees, the fans and the various other stakeholders of Rangers Football Club."

Mr Green was not for budging and rebuffed the offer from the Smith consortium, which undoubtedly led to more turbulence that summer. However, he not only came through it, he managed to persuade Walter Smith to join him and, indeed, on 11 November it was confirmed that the legendary manager had returned to the club to take up a role as a non-executive director along with Ian Hart, who had been a leading light in the Blue Knights consortium who also vied with Green's group for control.

So why the change of heart? Smith said, "Charles Green asked me if I would come back and join the board. At first I wasn't too sure because having been a manager I wasn't sure if I would fit in to the boardroom. My only previous involvement in that area was giving a manager's report at board meetings.

"It took me a while to find out what my responsibilities would be but Charles kept saying, 'Come on, you need to come in and help us.' He felt I could have

There was a united front on 11 November when Walter Smith returned to Rangers to become a non-executive director, while Ian Hart also joined the board in the same role just a matter of months after both men had been involved in consortia which were rivals to Charles Green's.

an input that would help the club and that was the most important thing.

"I was involved with Jim McColl and Douglas Park, who were interested in taking over the club, and they asked me to front their bid. When that didn't happen and Charles' consortium was successful, then everyone involved in the other consortium – Jim, Douglas and I – wished them every success. The club's well-being was the most important thing.

"I think once Charles got his feet under the table everyone was impressed by the manner in which he handled the takeover, especially in the early part. I don't think it would have mattered who the owners were, there was always going to be a bit of scepticism after Craig Whyte. However, he has gone a long way to winning everybody over – including myself – and when he asked me to help I was pleased to do so."

The appointment of Smith and Hart was another massive moment for Green and Rangers as they continued to build towards the share issue and, significantly, it gave Ally McCoist a close ally on the board. Of course McCoist was thrilled with the news, as were all of the staff at Murray Park, and there is little doubt the appointment had a calming influence on all concerned.

There was more good news on 20 November – although it was of the bittersweet variety. Rangers won 'the Big Tax Case' when the First Tier Tax Tribunal ruled that tax was not liable on the EBTs operated and that they were deemed to be loans. If only this verdict had come out before Craig Whyte appeared on the scene then the calamitous collapse of the club may not have happened.

Supporters were pleased but also angry after the constant assumption and assertion by many that Rangers were guilty. There is also no question that confidential information was leaked into the public domain and the Murray Group, who administered the EBTs, called for a thorough and far-reaching investigation. Of course, pragmatically the verdict meant nothing to newco other than the considerable fact that the SPL had launched a commission into whether the use of EBTs contravened their rules.

Ally McCoist called for it to be scrapped. He said, "I would be extremely hopeful that perhaps common sense would now prevail and they would drop it. That would be the ideal situation so that we could all start moving forward again. All you want is an opportunity to start again and move forward

Top left: The Rangers players have often heard their team being referred to as the Queen's XI and they found out it was true at the Charity Foundation's Best of British Ball on 3 November. Pictured with the 'Monarch' (impersonator Mary Reynolds) are Lewis Macleod, Andy Mitchell, Kal Naismith, Kevin Kyle, Kyle Hutton, Barrie McKay and Dean Shiels.

Top middle: Dean Shiels was a two-goal hero for Rangers in the 7–0 thrashing of Alloa in the third round of the Scottish Cup on 3 November.

Top right: Barrie McKay was also at the double in the big win over Paul Hartley's side with two great strikes towards the end of the match.

Ibrox looks majestic in this panoramic shot of the stadium ahead of the emotional Remembrance scenes which surrounded the meeting with Peterhead on 10 November.

Top left: Troops from 207 Battery fired an L118 artillery gun to mark the start of the minute's silence for Remembrance at Ibrox on 10 November.

Bottom left: There was poignancy at Ibrox as the players of Rangers and Peterhead remained silent in front of an incredible poppy display in the Govan Stand.

and if they were to do that it would certainly be closure on that point and we could start again."

His call for common sense fell on deaf ears and the commission, which is thought to have cost £500,000, carried on to its conclusion in March. The fact that the conclusion would prove to be favourable only validated McCoist, but more of that in Chapter 8.

On the field it was a good month for the manager, as Rangers took Alloa Athletic apart on 3 November by winning 7–0 at Ibrox in the third round of the Scottish Cup, with Dean Shiels, Lee McCulloch and Barrie McKay all netting doubles and Robbie Crawford also getting in on the act. It was cathartic to say the least after the bitter disappointment of losing to Inverness in the League Cup four days earlier.

A week later the scenes at Ibrox were something special to behold as an incredible card display was operated by the supporters as part of the Remembrance activity and hundreds of servicemen and women came onto the pitch at half-time to rapturous applause. It was another massive crowd with 48,407 in attendance, and they watched Rangers win three league games in a row for the first time that season when goals from Lee McCulloch and Lee Wallace were enough to defeat Peterhead.

It was an emotional day for Andy Jenkinson from Leeds, who was a lapsed Rangers fan who returned to follow his team as a result of the turmoil surrounding the club. Andy said, "I was living in Cumbria and a few of us started following Rangers when Graeme Souness took over and started the revolution and we followed them for about seven years. Then we started to get married, have children and move away so we drifted away from Rangers. I don't think I saw the team for about twelve years but when we started to have all the trouble I felt it was time to come back.

"My first game was the Peterhead game in November and I couldn't have picked a better game because of the fantastic

Top right: Pipers led the servicemen and women onto the Ibrox playing surface at half-time with the Marines at the front.

Bottom right: The Ibrox legions showed their support to the soldiers who have fought so bravely for the UK in conflicts all over the world.

poppy display, the Union flags and the gun going off. It was so emotional to be back at Ibrox and that was me back into it again. I think we have all seen how the terrible events have galvanised the Rangers fans and I'm delighted to be part of it.

"It's a fantastic institution, a fantastic football club and I love it. It's a lot of miles and a lot of hours following Rangers, but it's worth it."

On 17 November Rangers racked up a 6–2 victory over East Stirlingshire at Ochilview, with McCulloch hitting another double. Andy Little, Lee Wallace and Kal Naismith were also on target, while Kevin Kyle scored his first goal for the club. A week later Rangers should have been travelling to Moray in the north of Scotland to take on Elgin at Borough Briggs, but the match was called off on the Friday night when it was discovered that extra tickets had been printed and sold and crowd safety could not be guaranteed. It smacked of trying to maximise on Rangers' visit and the SFL acted quickly by fining Elgin £25,000 and severely censuring them, while also ordering them to pay Rangers' costs.

Of course, many fans had made plans for a weekend in the Highlands. For example, Graham Clelland and Maggie Tennant were already on a train to Inverness when they heard the news that the game was off. However, having already booked their hotel, they decided to stay there for the weekend anyway – and they were not alone. Embarrassingly for Elgin, their very next match was going to be against Rangers at Ibrox on 2 December after the two sides had been paired in the fourth round of the Scottish Cup.

Overall it was a brilliant month for Northern Ireland defender Chris Hegarty, who had come into the side towards the end of October and kept his place, whether it was at full-back or in the centre of defence. He savoured being part of the victories, but there is little doubt that the 10 November game with Peterhead will live long in the young man's memory.

Chris said, "The Alloa result was a really good one for us and I remember at that time just being delighted to be in the team, it was fantastic for me.

"That was the start of our eleven-game winning run and it was an important stage of the season for us. The Remembrance Day game at Ibrox against Peterhead was something special and it's probably my highlight of the year. My brother Barry was on the pitch that day and the stadium was packed, so it was just a fantastic occasion. I spoke to some of his mates after the game and they were just over the moon to go out in front of the fans at half-time, it meant so much to them.

"I've been in the situation where I don't know what is going to happen to my brother, so fair play to those guys for what they do and I have so much respect for them. It was great to get the 2–0 win for them and our fans that day, especially against Peterhead, who we know are a very good team. Big Jig got the opener, even although he was playing at centre-half alongside me, and then Lee Wallace scored later in the game.

"So that was a really pleasing day overall, and then we went to East Stirling and won 6–2. I remember Barrie McKay played

really well and we were always favourites to come out on top after they had a man sent off after the half-hour mark.

"After that we were disappointed to concede two goals, which made it 2–1 and 3–2 respectively, but we then shifted through the gears with Kevin Kyle and Kal Naismith taking their goals well before Jig scored his second from the penalty spot.

"Credit has to go to East Stirlingshire for the hard work they put in that day, but we were pleased to record another win before going into a busy December."

So with Walter Smith back at the club and lifelong fan Ian Hart also on the board the supporters were undoubtedly more comfortable that the club was in a more stable position to push ahead with the recovery process. Of equal importance was the message that it sent out to potential investors. Encouraging the return of Smith was definitely one of the shrewdest moves that Green made.

Top left: The armed services reciprocated and seemed genuinely thrilled to get the chance to be on the pitch at Ibrox.

Top middle: Sandy Jardine and assistant manager Kenny McDowall proudly posed with the armed forces members ahead of the Remembrance activity at Ibrox on 10 November.

Top right: It was a day to remember for these soldiers as they soaked up the atmosphere at Ibrox.

Top: Ian Black celebrated with Lee Wallace after the full-back drove in the second goal to clinch the win against Peterhead.

Right: Lee McCulloch took his goals tally for the season to nineteen when he opened the scoring against Peterhead on 10 November.

Lee McCulloch led Rangers into the 'arena' at Ochilview for the clash with East Stirlingshire. Notice how the Stenhousemuir crest above the tunnel had been covered with a black and white flag!

Kit controller Jimmy Bell got the strips ready for the game with East Stirlingshire on 17 November at Stenhousemuir's Ochilview ground, where the dressing rooms were rather cramped, to say the least.

As ever, the Rangers fans turned out in their numbers to fill the Ochilview ground, including a group from Oban.

The weather was not the best when Rangers visited Ochilview but these fans were certainly in the mood to back their team.

Left: A special 'friendship' scarf was made up for the occasion but Rangers were not too friendly as they raced to a 6–2 win over the Shire.

Above: Andy Little celebrated his strike against East Stirlingshire which would undoubtedly have made Captain Walter Barrie proud. Rangers wore black armbands in his memory after he was killed in action in Afghanistan just six days earlier.

LEST WE FORGET FROM ALL AT RANGERS F.C.

This Wreath was made by Disabled ex-servicemen in
Lady Haig's Poppy Factory, Edinburgh

Top far left: The away dressing room at Ochilview from another angle also shows that life in the bottom tier was a far cry from Ibrox and the top stadia of Europe that Rangers were used to.

Top left: Captain marvel Lee McCulloch was on the spot twice against East Stirlingshire when he converted two penalties in the 6–2 win.

Bottom far left: Rangers paid their respects to the fallen when chairman Malcolm Murray laid a wreath at the John Greig statue ahead of the Peterhead game on 10 November. Also representing the club were Supporters' Liaison Officer Jim Hannah, Sandy Jardine, Charles Green, Ally McCoist and Brian Stockbridge.

Bottom left: A close-up of the wreath laid by Malcolm Murray in tribute to all of those who have lost their lives serving their country.

Above: Ally McCoist showed the way in training at Murray Park, with Ian Black and Fraser Aird following the boss's every move.

Top right: Rangers are always in the spotlight and Ally McCoist faced the media every week – sometimes twice a week.

Right: Some of the greatest names in Rangers' history got together with Robbie Crawford (back left) and lifelong supporter Andy Bain (front second right) in November to help promote a celebration of 140 years of the club at the Stirling Albion game on 8 December. Back: Robbie Crawford, Charlie Miller, Alex Rae, Derek Johnstone, Alex MacDonald, Willie Johnston. Front: Willie Henderson, Ian McMillan, Sandy Jardine, Andy Bain, Davie Wilson.

Graeme Souness was responsible for revolutionising Rangers in 1986 and was delighted to check out a special celebration of the 140 years of the club at the Scottish Football Museum where he featured prominently.

Chapter 6
December Will Be Magic

IF YOU seek counsel from any leading City analyst about investing in football he will invariably tell you that it would be more prudent to stick your cash on an outsider in the three o'clock race at Uttoxeter. Recent history has shown that ploughing capital into a football club is not the smartest move if you are looking for a significant return. To that end, much scorn was poured on Charles Green's plan to list Rangers on the AIM market through an IPO, and there was considerable scepticism that he would get anywhere near the £20 million he was hoping to raise. Of course, there were those who just wanted it to fail. However, the cynics were forced to skulk away and eat their words as over £22 million was raised on 17 December, with £5 million of it coming from supporters. It was a runaway success and it gave Rangers the capital it needed to continue the recovery process. Just ten months after the toxic chaos of the Craig Whyte days, Rangers were debt-free and had plenty of cash in the bank – something few if any clubs in the UK could claim.

Green said at the time, "This is an exciting time for everyone associated with this 140-year-old institution, but we are just at the start of the Journey. We are rebuilding and Rangers will rise again, and we will do so with the help of our fans and the institutional investors who are on board.

"This process has generated over £22 million, which has exceeded the figure of £20 million that we set out to raise when we announced our intention to float the company on 11 October 2012.

"I would like to thank our supporters who stepped up to the plate when asked to buy season tickets earlier in the season and have done so again at a time of year when money is extremely tight. I think it's important for people to understand that the reason the institutions invested their money so readily was because they saw the Rangers fans. They saw 40–50,000 turning up at Ibrox, and that is what people have invested in. It's not just Charles Green and Ally McCoist – we were only telling the story – it's about Rangers and its fans, the history and tradition.

"If we think back to when people said fans wouldn't support Charles Green, well, they have. We were then told that institutions wouldn't buy shares and they have. We've now exceeded all expectations and this is an historic moment for this club, and the club has never been in this position."

It was undoubtedly the zenith of Green's time with the club, and regardless of what people may think of him, he deserves credit for this achievement.

Brian Stockbridge, Ally McCoist and Charles Green were thrilled to receive a special plaque by the London Stock Exchange on the highly successful listing on the AIM Market.

Press Association

Top left: A panoramic view of the magnificent scenes at Ibrox on 8 December when Rangers officially celebrated their 140th year. The four young men who started the club in 1872 – Moses McNeil, Peter McNeil, Peter Campbell and William McBeath – could never have imagined they gave birth to such an institution.

Bottom left: Ibrox was specially illuminated with red, white and blue lighting as part of the 140-year celebrations.

Above: Rangers legends in the Blue Room to celebrate the 140th anniversary of the club. Back row (left to right): Graham Fyfe, Alfie Conn, Ally Dawson, Andy Goram, Mark Hateley, Marvin Andrews, Richard Gough, Michael Mols, Lorenzo Amoruso, Alan McLaren, Charlie Miller, Gordon Durie, Mark Walters, Dave McPherson. Middle row: Andy Gray, Jim Denny, Colin Stein, Dave Smith, Willie Mathieson, Tom Forsyth, Derek Johnstone, Gordon Smith, Colin Jackson, John MacDonald, Johnny Hamilton, Willie Johnston, Quinton Young, Billy Semple, Bobby Russell. Front row: Ronnie McKinnon, Tommy McLean, Willie Henderson, Jim Forrest, Bobby Brown, Johnny Hubbard, Harold Davis, Eric Caldow and Davie Wilson.

Indeed, December in general was a magical month for Rangers as the team recorded seven victories in succession, six of them coming in SFL 3, which meant they marched into 2013 with a 15-point lead, and the reality was the title was already in the bag.

There were also fantastic scenes at Ibrox on 8 December when 140 years of history was celebrated in style, when a host of legendary figures were roared onto the field by another world record crowd of 49,813. It was particularly pleasing for the supporters to see the Greatest Ever Ranger John Greig walk onto the field proudly holding the European Cup Winners' Cup that he and the other Barcelona Bears won on 24 May 1972. The legendary captain had not been back at the club since resigning from the board along with John McClelland in November 2011, when the two of them were effectively ostracised by Craig Whyte.

He said, "I accepted the invitation to celebrate the club's 140th birthday because I respect the club so much. I also didn't want to be disrespectful to any of my colleagues or the staff that I've worked with throughout the years. Last of all, I wanted to thank the supporters for all of the tremendous support that they've given me throughout the last fifty years. It was great to be back."

Some fantastic Rangers players were there, from Bobby Brown and Johnny Hubbard in the immediate post-War years, through '60s stars like Willie Henderson, Davie Wilson and Ronnie McKinnon, to nine-in-a-row heroes like Richard Gough, Andy Goram and Mark Hateley, and recent favourites Jörg Albertz, Lorenzo Amoruso and Davie Weir.

There was one glaring absentee – Sandy Jardine. He had announced the previous month that he was being treated

Left: The Rangers fans showed their support for the legendary Sandy Jardine after it was revealed he was being treated for cancer. Since the news broke, they offered applause for him on the second minute of every home match.

Right: Lifelong Rangers fan and media pundit Andy Gray – who had a short spell at Ibrox – was thrilled to compere the festivities at the 140 celebrations and had fun with the greatest of them all, John Greig, who was joined by fellow Cup Winners' Cup heroes Colin Stein, Derek Johnstone (partially hidden), Willie Johnston, Willie Mathieson, Willie Henderson, Ronnie McKinnon and Dave Smith.

Bottom right: John Greig had not been back at Ibrox since resigning from the board in November 2011, but the skipper of the Cup Winners' Cup team and the only man to appear in three Treble-winning sides just had to be at the 140 years celebrations.

for cancer and he was too unwell to attend the event. Few men exude the Rangers spirit in the way that Sandy Jardine does and few have conducted themselves with such dignity in a near fifty-year association with the club. He was an exceptional footballer during a fifteen-year top-team playing career and he has also been a magnificent ambassador for the club. However, perhaps his greatest achievement has been the inspiration and leadership he showed in 2012 when the club he loves was nearly destroyed. When Rangers were floundering and rudderless as the horror of administration began to kick in, Jardine and manager Ally McCoist were the two men who stepped up to the plate. As Craig Whyte grabbed his coat and fled the parish and the bean-counters moved in, there was an air of bewilderment and confusion. Jardine sought to ease fears, seek clarity and drive the recovery process in all aspects, and everyone at Ibrox will be forever grateful to him for doing so.

In the opening game of December – a Scottish Cup tie with Elgin which Rangers won 3–0, with goals from Dean Shiels, Kevin Kyle and Kal Naismith – the supporters burst into applause on the two-minute mark to show their respect given that he invariably wore the No.2 jersey. McCoist certainly missed having him as a sounding board as much as anything and looks forward to the day when they work together again. He said, "Sandy was religiously in all the time and he would sit down, have a cup of tea, we'd moan at each other and he'd ask me how I was going to approach things. He was great to bounce ideas off, really first class. With the greatest of respect,

Harold Davis is proud to have played for two great Rangers teams – the late 1950s and the early 1960s – and he led out former teammates Davie Wilson and Eric Caldow onto the Ibrox pitch, carrying the elegant Glasgow Cup.

How much would this group of legends be worth in today's market? Jim Forrest (holding the Scottish Cup), Eric Caldow, Davie Wilson, Harold Davis, Johnny Hubbard and Bobby Brown enjoy their day at Ibrox.

Lorenzo Amoruso and Michael Mols were both involved in nightmare journeys due to the weather to get from their homes in Italy and Holland to the Ibrox celebrations, but they were never going to miss them.

Andy Gray had a laugh with the goalie Andy Goram, who clutched the SPL trophy while Mark Walters and Dave McPherson enjoyed the ambience at the 140 years celebrations.

Gordon Smith and Tom Forsyth were key men in the famous 1977/78 Treble season when they swept all before them. The League Cup, carried by Tom, was special for Gordon, as he headed the winner in the final against Celtic.

Richard Gough proudly clutches the Scottish Football League championship trophy, which Rangers famously won nine seasons in succession. Gough was skipper for seven of them.

Sandy knew the club as well as anybody. He was hurting as much as anybody, but at the same time, he was sensible enough to take a different viewpoint on things and that was very, very important. I was right in the face of things, whereas he was up the hill and looking down at what was happening from further away.

"We're talking now about a football club and people's jobs but what's happened to Sandy puts everything into perspective. I can't wait to have him back here. It would be wrong just to say that for myself because everyone within Murray Park misses him. His health will indicate when he comes back, but this place will be a far better one when that door gets kicked open and Sandy comes in." As you will see in Chapter 9, Sandy was back at Ibrox in March during a break in his treatment and he received a fantastic ovation from the fans.

Rangers won their game on 8 December when they beat Stirling Albion 2–0 with second-half goals from David Templeton, making his first start since his ankle problem, and Andy Little. The following week they won 4–2 at Montrose when one Rangers supporter gave strict instructions to home-side substitute David Gray not to score – and he promptly ignored her! Lloyd Young's flicked finish on fifteen minutes gave Montrose a shock lead, but Lee McCulloch equalised from the penalty spot to make the score level at half-time and Rangers seemed to be in a comfortable position when Kevin Kyle and Dean Shiels gave them a 3–1 lead. On came Gray and Rangers fanatic Agnes Douglas had a quick word with him when he came across to take a throw-in – but her psychology did not work.

She said, "I normally stand at the front when I go to the away matches and I have managed to get to speak to some of the opposition players and they have been very friendly. I was at the Montrose game and we were leading 3–1 when their

Top right: Two legends together, Richard Gough and John Greig, are undoubtedly two of the greatest captains in the 140-year history of Rangers.

Middle right: The old and the not so old – Michael Mols was thrilled to share the Ibrox pitch with 1960s stars Davie Wilson and Eric Caldow.

Bottom right: Derek Johnstone was only eighteen when he played in the Cup Winners' Cup Final and he proudly walked out at Ibrox with his teammates from that glorious period.

Guests were treated to some fantastic stories from the legends at the 140 Celebrations Dinner. Michael Mols addressed the audience as Lorenzo Amoruso, Mark Hateley and Mark Walters looked on.

super sub came on. I told him he better not score, and then he curled one into the top corner!"

Agnes and her fellow travelling fans had their hearts in their mouths when Garry Wood struck the crossbar and Scott Johnston hit the post very late on. Thankfully Robbie Crawford made sure of the victory with a fine finish in injury-time.

Lee Wallace was sent off for denying a goal-scoring opportunity against Annan on 18 December, but the Galabank side missed the penalty and Rangers went on to win 3–0 despite only having ten men. Elgin City were hammered 6–2 in the match, which had to be rearranged after the ticket shambles of the previous month, then Clyde were rather comfortably taken care of on Boxing Day when Rangers won 3–0 at Ibrox.

The final match of the year was another remarkable occasion. Queen's Park's average attendance for the season had been a little over 500. When Rangers went to Hampden on 29 December the crowd was 30,017. This was the equivalent of nearly three and a half seasons of paying customers for the Spiders. No wonder the SFL 3 embraced Rangers with open arms. In the end, it was teenage Canadian Fraser Aird who snatched victory for Rangers with a low shot in the dying moments.

It had been a good month on the field and key to the success was young midfielder Lewis Macleod, who had emerged as a player who was never off Ally McCoist's team sheet. Macleod relished the 140 Celebration game in particular. He said, "That was an unbelievable day for everyone at the club and as a young player it was exciting to see so many legends coming back to Ibrox. Walking out the tunnel was a great feeling, as it always is, but we had to make sure we stayed focused and kept our good run going. We managed to do that, with Temps and Andy Little scoring on the day, and it was good for us to get a bit of revenge after our defeat to them at Forthbank at the start of October.

Top left: Lee McCulloch slammed home a penalty at Montrose but it proved to be a difficult day at Links Park before Rangers finally prevailed.

Bottom left: Robbie Crawford belied his inexperience with a superbly cool finish in the final moments of the 15 December clash at Montrose to clinch a 4–2 win.

Right: Andy Little celebrated his strike against Annan Athletic on 18 December as relentless Rangers started to pull away at the top of SFL 3.

Bottom right: He is normally a creator but David Templeton struck twice against Annan in a 3–0 win, even though Rangers were down to ten men.

"But after the Stirling game we went to Montrose and won 4–2 on their 3G surface. It was a tricky game up there and at 3–2 they hit the bar right at the death, which might have given them a draw but we went up the other end and wee Robbie got our fourth.

"The games were coming thick and fast at that stage, and next up we faced Annan at Ibrox on a Tuesday night. Temps scored a couple, but I remember Lee Wallace was sent off just before the hour mark and the ref pointed to the spot. Thankfully Neil Alexander made a good save from Scott Chaplain's penalty and we then managed to get two more goals from Temps and Andy Little, despite being down to ten men.

"That result meant we kept building momentum through the festive period, and on 22 December we travelled up to Borough Briggs and put in one of our best away displays against Elgin, and I was delighted to score in a 6–2 win.

"We then got another win on Boxing Day against Clyde before wee Fraser got his goal in the last minute at Hampden, which meant we finished the month on a high. Unfortunately I missed that game at the national stadium due to an illness. I was gutted because I was desperate to play in that one. So many Rangers fans went along to the game, and although we maybe weren't at our best, it was great to see Fraser get his first goal for the club."

So Rangers leapt into 2013 in terrific shape both on and off the field.

Top left: These four ladies showed their true colours when they followed Rangers to Montrose on 15 December.

Middle left: A blue Santa was full of festive cheer as he made the journey to Links Park to give Rangers his backing.

Bottom left: The Rangers fans were proud to show their colours on their travels and this couple even decorated their car for the journey to Elgin.

Above: The rearranged game with Elgin City went ahead on 22 December, and these three lads from Bellshill were there to see Rangers win 6–2.

Top right: These five fans were in early at Borough Briggs to book a decent place on the small terracing to follow the team against Elgin.

Bottom right: With Christmas only three days away, these three lads got into the Yuletide spirit ahead of the Elgin game at Borough Briggs.

Left: Lewis Macleod was a top performer for Rangers in the first half of the season and he got a lift from Andy Little after scoring in the 6–2 win over Elgin.

Above: Andy Little bagged two goals in the game with Elgin to maintain his terrific strike rate for the season. He would eventually claim twenty-five goals in all.

Top right: December was a prolific period for David Templeton as he scored four times in the month, including this one against Clyde.

Right: There was no Boxing Day hangover for Rangers as they eased past Clyde 3–0, with Lee Wallace on target.

Above: It seemed like a cup final day when Rangers went to Hampden on 29 December with thousands descending on the national stadium for the league clash with Queen's Park.

Right: Queen's Park v. Rangers is the original Glasgow derby and one of the oldest in world football but these two seasoned Queen's fans were more than friendly to their young Rangers counterpart.

Opposite: It was one of the most exciting moments of the season when teenage winger Fraser Aird cut in from the left and fired a low right-foot shot into the corner of the Queen's Park net in the final seconds of the 29 December clash at Hampden to send Rangers 15 points clear at the top of SFL 3.

The scoreboard at the packed Rangers end of Hampden tells the story.

Chapter 7
New Year Blues

RANGERS FANS became sick of hearing the expression 'sporting integrity' during a summer of discontent in 2012, mainly because of the gross hypocrisy of those who regularly used it. Their pet hate phrase for 2013 was 'league reconstruction' as Scottish football procrastinated, argued, put self-interest before the greater good and the saga frustratingly dragged on. In January, however, the topic was of a much more serious nature as it directly affected Rangers in a detrimental way and generally the plan hatched by the SPL seemed infinitely more complex than it needed to be.

The top-flight clubs came up with a proposal to change the structure from 12-10-10-10 to three divisions of twelve, twelve and eighteen. The complex part was that the two twelves would split into three eights after two rounds of matches. The top eight would play for the title and European places, the middle eight would play for four places in the following season's top flight and the bottom eight would play to avoid relegation to the eighteen.

The detrimental part was that Rangers would be in the eighteen – in other words, they would remain in the bottom tier of the game even though they were heading towards the SFL 3 championship and therefore expected promotion. Ally McCoist and Charles Green spoke vociferously against the proposals and indeed offered an alternative plan of 14-14-14, which would include play-offs between the divisions.

McCoist said, "Everyone keeps talking to us about sporting integrity so I might as well bring it up myself. You can't possibly move the goalposts during a season. I think the vast majority of the footballing public, the fans included, are probably in agreement we need change. But you can't have change during a season, I wouldn't have thought. By all means, have it at the end of a season or plan them for the start of a new one. You can't move the goalposts and effectively waste people's seasons, if you like. If it goes ahead and starts next season, this season is meaningless to a lot of teams.

"At this moment it is hypothetical because nothing has been agreed, but I would hope the public would agree this should be done at a time that suits everybody. During the season is certainly not a time to be talking about doing that for the following season, far from it.

"How can you be aiming for promotion at the start of a season then still be in the bottom league if you earn promotion? That's the argument against it and

As ever, Rangers were box office wherever they travelled and Annan Athletic relished a second visit from the Glasgow giants on 2 January.

why you can't possibly go changing things during the season. If it went through, there would be no point in us playing at the moment and what a slap in the face that would be to everyone else in SFL3, including our fans and our players. Our supporters have been slapped right on the coupon at every opportunity and that's unbelievable. Do you know something? All it will do is make them stronger, I know it will. It will make us all stronger and that's fine.

"This isn't a strop where I'm throwing the toys out of the pram. I just feel if this goes through it will be another slap in the face to our supporters. Hopefully common sense will prevail and the people who are playing for cups and leagues are duly rewarded.

"My own personal view would be that if they're going to make any changes, make them the following year. My gripe is moving goalposts during a season is not ideal and there are people in the SFA who have backed me up on that. In an ideal world, if we are lucky enough to get promoted I would expect promotion from our league."

Green was equally scathing of the plans. He said, "If this does happen what is the point of us finishing the season? We might as well have a winter break now till next August. I can't see any point in carrying on with meaningless matches.

"In what league do you win a division and then end up playing the same teams again the following season? There is no meaning to it, in reality. I haven't read anything other than what is in the press and if that is what we have sat here eagerly awaiting to transform Scottish football, my advice to the board of Rangers is the quicker we can leave Scottish football the better. I can't see anything that is going to transform the finances, the status or the excitement."

Of course, there was and remains no exit route from Scottish football. Green was trying to make a point.

Top: John Greig was the captain on the fateful day and he sent his own personal message attached to a floral tribute.

Bottom: A short service was held at the John Greig Statue on 2 January to commemorate the terrible Ibrox Disaster in 1971 when sixty-six Rangers fans lost their lives.

There is little doubt that the reconstruction debate cast a shadow over this stage of the season. Coincidentally perhaps, the team's form dipped during the month and they were held at home by Elgin City and Montrose when, on both occasions, they had been profligate in front of goal. Skipper Lee McCulloch missed virtually the whole month with a foot problem, and then there was a serious knee injury to the highly talented Lewis Macleod which ruled him out until the final fixture, while Darren Cole's season was finished almost as soon as it had started when he suffered an ankle problem, which required surgery, in his only start of the campaign at Annan.

The month had started well at Galabank on 2 January when Rangers won 3–1, and it was a particularly good day for David Templeton, who had been badly injured on his first visit there in only the second game of his Rangers career on 15 September. He scored twice and the first goal was an audacious chip from a tight angle, which fooled the goalkeeper and fell in at the far post, while the second was a long-range deflected effort.

Prior to travelling to the Borders, manager Ally McCoist and club officials attended a short service at the John Greig Statue at Ibrox in memory of the sixty-six victims who died at the Disaster on 2 January 1971 when an horrific crush developed on stairway 13 at the conclusion of the traditional New Year derby with Celtic.

Tradition is very important at Rangers, and as usual the Loving Cup ceremony took place in the Blue Room at Ibrox ahead of the opening home game of 2013 on 5 January when Elgin City were the visitors. The stunning piece of memorabilia is one of only thirty cast from a unique mould to commemorate the coronation of King George VI in May 1937. Normally housed in the Trophy Room at Ibrox, the story of how it came into Rangers' possession is part of the club's folklore and a long-standing part of the club's history.

Top left: Rangers were in need of inspiration at Annan with the score tied at 1–1, and Robbie Crawford provided it with a well-executed finish.

Above: The Murray Park kid celebrated his vital strike and Rangers went on to win 3–1. David Templeton scored the second of his two goals.

Left: Sadly the Annan match was a nightmare for defender Darren Cole, who was carried off with an ankle injury and did not play again in the season.

Opposite: Lewis Macleod celebrated his third goal of the season with a strike against Elgin City at Ibrox on 8 January, but it turned into a difficult day for the Light Blues.

Identical Loving Cups were presented to each of the twenty-two English First Division clubs of the time. Others went to the British Museum and other organisations. Stoke City were one of the recipients and it was when the Light Blues were asked to take part in a fund-raising match that the Potteries side handed over theirs as a gift. Then managed by Bill Struth, Rangers had been invited to play in a game to generate money for the families of miners who lost their lives in the Holditch Colliery Disaster. City's president, Sir Francis Joseph, handed over his team's Loving Cup as a way of expressing thanks following a 0–0 draw between the sides. It was given to the Glasgow outfit on the proviso that the vessel be used in perpetuity to toast the reigning monarch prior to the club's first home match of every new year. To this day, that tradition has been maintained by the Rangers directors and their visiting counterparts, and the 2013 ceremony was shown on the giant screens at half-time.

The fans enjoyed seeing that, but they did not enjoy Rangers' performance, which finished horribly when goalkeeper Neil Alexander inadvertently allowed the ball to slip through his hands and into the net to give Elgin a 1–1 draw.

The following week was an emotional rollercoaster for the supporters as they watched their side race to a 3–0 lead against Berwick Rangers on 12 January and then proceed to give away two terrible goals. Andy Little eased the tension with a fine left-foot finish, which clinched his second hat-trick of the season, having scored twice in the first half, with Templeton netting the other. The players were oblivious to a tragedy in the stadium that day when fifty-seven-year-old Rab Learmonth from Port Seton in East Lothian collapsed in the Broomloan Stand and later died, just four days after his father Nicol had passed away. In the next match at Peterhead the players wore black armbands as a mark of respect.

It was another tough day for the team at Balmoor on 20 January in more ways than one, as the committed Peterhead players never gave Rangers any time on the ball. In the end Sandaza's second goal of the season was enough to separate the sides. The football result might have been disappointing for Peterhead chairman Rodger Morrison, but the financial rewards of having Rangers in the same league were huge.

He said, "It still seems unreal that Rangers were in the Third Division at all. They had a huge impact from an excitement point of view, a media point of view and a financial point of view. It's been great for every club in the Third Division. Playing Rangers twice made a big difference to us and we maximised the opportunity by putting up marquees for corporate use as well as selling out the stadium because we knew it might be our only chance to get two visits from Rangers."

The final match of the month, a 1–1 draw at Ibrox with Montrose on 26 January, was a huge disappointment to manager McCoist, not just because Montrose equalised in the final minute with a stunning David Gray strike, but due to the lethargic performance. McCoist is usually calm in these situations but he revealed his true feelings when asked about the supporters displaying their displeasure at the end. He said, "I would have booed myself. That's as angry as I've ever been since I became manager. The players better switch on quick or they'll be switched off completely. That should act as a wake-up call. That level won't be tolerated."

Despite their patchy performances, Rangers ended up finishing the month with a healthier advantage than at the start of it, as they opened up a 19-point lead. Another positive was Lee Wallace filling in for Lee McCulloch while the captain attempted to recover from his foot problem. It was a period the former Hearts defender thoroughly enjoyed. He said, "It was great and I loved deputising for big Jig as captain. I felt it did add a bit of extra responsibility on my shoulders,

The Rangers supporters show their backing for the legendary Sandy Jardine,
who was in the midst of treatment for cancer.

Top left: The elegant Loving Cup is undoubtedly one of the most ornate and interesting items of memorabilia which are housed in the Ibrox Trophy Room.

Above: The Loving Cup ceremony – when the directors toast the reigning monarch – takes place at the first home game of every new year, and here club historian David Mason explained the story to the Blue Room guests as Charles Green, Ally McCoist and Malcolm Murray looked on.

Left: As is tradition, all of the guests drink from the Loving Cup and manager Ally McCoist was first to sip the whisky ahead of the home match with Elgin City on 5 January.

Opposite top: It was no great surprise that Ally McCoist was named SFL 3 Manager of the Month for December given that Rangers had racked up an impressive run of six consecutive league victories.

Opposite bottom: There was no escaping the rough and tumble of life in SFL 3 as Lee Wallace showed his commitment in a challenge during the clash with Berwick on 12 January.

which was good, and I thrived on that. I knew I had to lead by example, albeit I'm not as vocal as Jig. But in terms of my performances, I always try to approach every game in the same way and give 100 per cent. So I really loved getting the chance to be the captain, but at the same time we all wanted Jig to get back as quickly as possible as he is a big player for us whether he is in defence, midfield or attack. He is the main man and the best man for that role, but whenever he is out I'm certainly ready to take that responsibility on because being captain is a great honour.

"For me it was a big moment in the season although it was disappointing to drop points against Elgin City and Montrose. Aside from that, we had good results at two tricky away venues at Annan and Peterhead, which took us nineteen points clear, and there was also Andy Little's hat-trick against Berwick at Ibrox as well.

"So at the end of the month we were in a great position at the top of the league, and although there was still a lot of hard work ahead we were looking forward to the games, and with our unbelievable fans behind us we were determined to get over the finish line as quickly as possible."

Unbelievable is right. Season ticket sales smashed through the 38,000 barrier and only Manchester United, Arsenal, Newcastle United and Manchester City could boast a higher home attendance average than Rangers.

David Templeton does not seem to score easy goals and he showed fantastic technique to fire a low volley into the Berwick net to put Rangers 3–0 up after he was picked out perfectly by Fran Sandaza, who had supplied the cross. Fittingly, Templeton sought out the Spaniard to offer his thanks.

Andy Little was a treble king for the second time in the season when he scored three times against Berwick on 12 January.

The wee Rangers had pegged the Light Blues back to 3–2 when Little eased the nerves with a fine left-foot finish to complete his hat-trick.

Rangers found it tough on their second visit to Peterhead on 20 January and they scraped through with a 1–0 win. It was Sandaza who scored the only goal and Andy Little and Lee Wallace raced to congratulate him.

The trip to Balmoor was certainly a fraught and frigid occasion for manager Ally McCoist, who is seen here bellowing instructions to his players.

The Rangers fans at Peterhead paid tribute to fellow fan Rab Learmonth, who tragically passed away the previous week after suffering a heart attack at the Berwick game, just four days after his father Nicol had died.

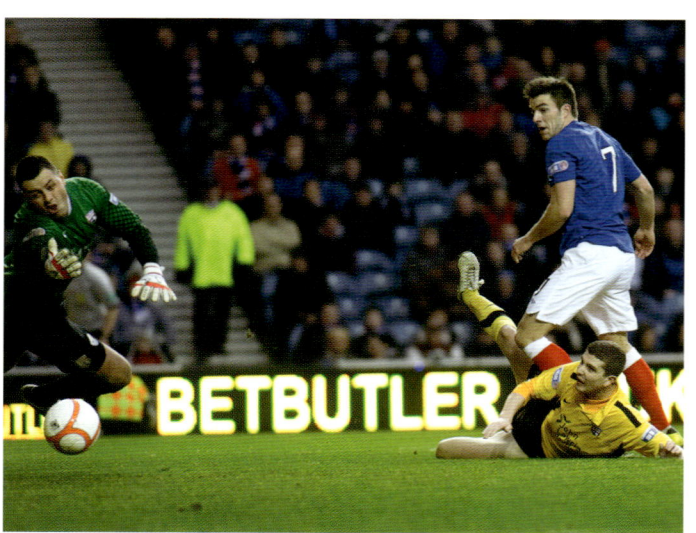

Rangers suffered more hometown blues on 26 January when Montrose came back to equalise and force a 1–1 draw. The Light Blues had taken the lead when luckless defender John Crawford deflected David Templeton's cross past keeper John Gibson, and Andy Little watched as the ball went into the net.

It might have been a tough and frustrating day against Montrose but these two girls were still keen on having fun.

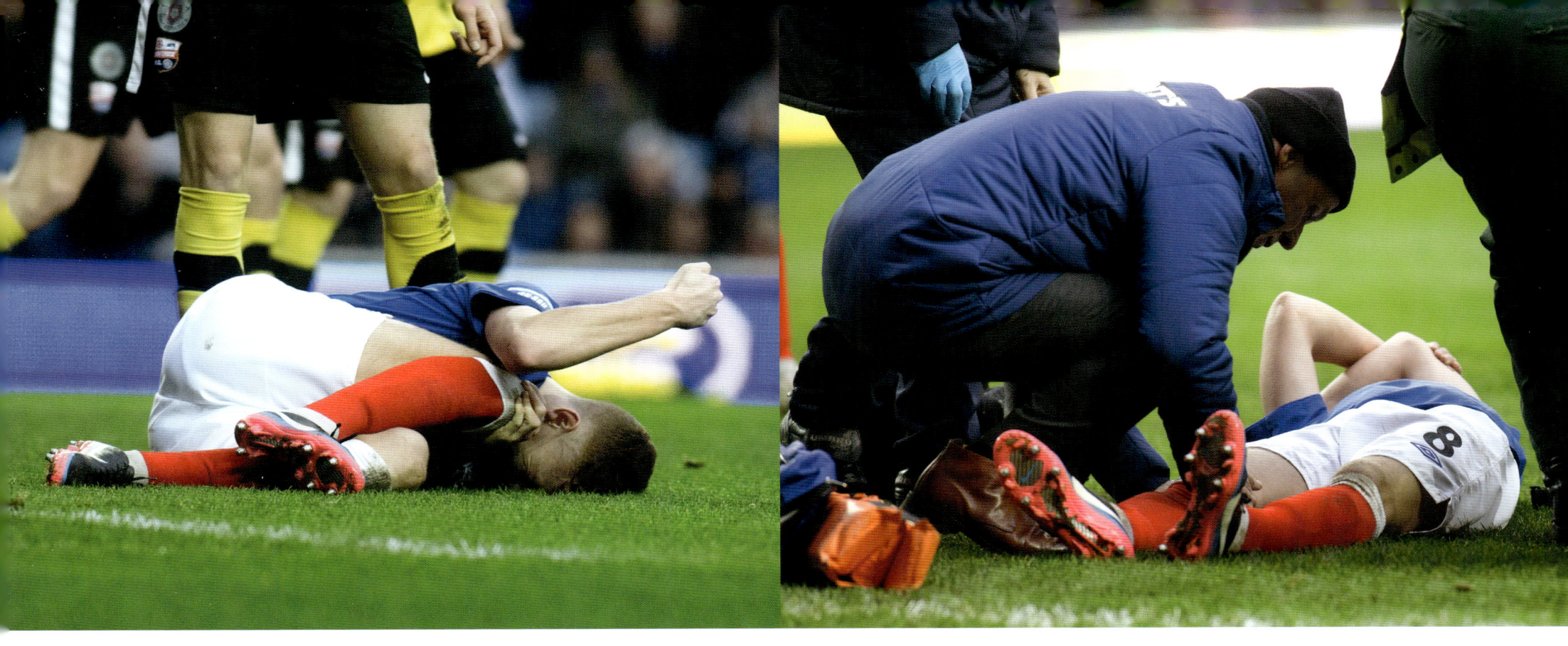

Top left: The desperately disappointing draw with Montrose was compounded by the fact that highly talented teenager Lewis Macleod suffered a bad knee injury when he was robustly challenged by Paul Watson.

Top right: Macleod, seen here being treated by club doctor Paul Jackson, suffered medial ligament damage and did not play again until the final match of the season. There is little doubt that Rangers missed his presence.

Top: There was a fair amount of controversy stirred when Rangers were drawn to play Dundee United in the Scottish Cup on 2 February and the fans at the Montrose game offered some encouragement for the impending Tannadice clash.

Bottom: Manager Ally McCoist made his feelings known on reconstruction to a press conference at Murray Park. He knew that a 12-12-18 format would be hugely detrimental to Rangers on so many levels.

Chapter 8
Sporting Integrity Intact

THE ANGER and resentment felt by Rangers supporters over the way the majority of SPL clubs acted during the summer of 2012 when trying to deal with the situation the Ibrox club had found itself in may take years to fully dissipate. Hiding under a banner of 'sporting integrity' the SPL clubs blocked Rangers from playing in the top division, claiming that their fans would boycott home games if the Light Blues were re-admitted to the top flight. Dundee United were one of the more prominent clubs in expressing their stance that Rangers should not be allowed back in to the SPL. Aberdeen and Hibs were also vocal and it seemed Rangers had few friends.

United's chairman, Stephen Thomson, was also a member of the SPL board that refused to take the responsibility of dealing with Rangers' application to 'rejoin' the SPL and opened it up to the clubs as a whole. He was also party to the original draft of the five-way agreement between the SPL, SFA, SFL, oldco and newco which sought to strip Rangers of the SPL titles won in 2003, 2005, 2009, 2010 and 2011 as a result of Rangers' usage of EBTs – even if it had not been proved that they had breached any football regulations. Going back slightly further, there was a dispute in 2009 when a match between Dundee United and Rangers was abandoned at half-time due to a water-logged pitch and fans were asked to retain their ticket stubs, but they were not offered refunds and had to pay again to watch the rearranged match.

So when Rangers were drawn to face Dundee United at Tannadice on 2 February in the fifth round of the Scottish Cup it re-opened old wounds. Rangers quickly decided they would not take tickets for the game and indeed urged all supporters not to purchase them from the Tayside club either. Remarkably, United tried to wriggle out of paying half of the gate money to Rangers, as is the SFA rule, and actually wrote to Rangers asking them to waive their right to the money. Charles Green told them to take a hike and then cutely indicated that Rangers would donate the cash to charity.

It was always going to be an arduous task for Ally McCoist's thrown-together squad to go to Tannadice and win. In the end it was not a lack of support that cost them – it was dreadful defending. United scored inside the first minute when Johnny Russell squirmed a shot under Neil Alexander, then Jon Daly, who will be plying his trade at Ibrox in the 2013/14 season, was completely unmarked to head a second goal on thirty-six minutes. A third goal eleven minutes from

Rangers fans were horrified that five of the world record 54 Scottish titles were under threat from the SPL Commission into the usage of EBTs and then delighted when the club was completely vindicated. When the news came through, Stevie Cochrane from the Ibrox maintenance team made sure the championship flags were gleaming.

Top far left: McCoist delivered his team talk to the players ahead of the controversial Scottish Cup tie against Dundee United after granting unprecedented access to the dressing room at Tannadice.

Bottom far left: Fran Sandaza was focused on his own thoughts while skipper for the day Lee Wallace and the rest of the team continued their preparations.

Top left: Wallace just needed another stretch before he got ready to lead the side out down the tunnel at Tannadice.

Bottom left: Manager Ally McCoist, as ever, was in a positive mood ahead of the Cup match on Tayside but it turned into a very difficult day for Rangers.

Above: The Rangers players got ready for Scottish Cup action against Dundee United on 2 February in a match that had dominated the headlines for contentious reasons.

time and needless red cards collected by Kal Naismith and Ian Black made it an awful day all-round.

However, the huge story of the month was the complete vindication of the usage of EBTs when the SPL Commission revealed its decision on 28 February. After a year or more of being repeatedly branded 'cheats' and worse by many sections of the media, it was proved that Rangers were no such thing. Not surprisingly, there was not a rash of apologies in newspapers, on radio stations on websites or on television by those who had spoken so passionately on EBTs. In their findings, the Commission, headed by Lord Nimmo Smith, stated, "Rangers FC did not gain any unfair competitive advantage from the contraventions of the SPL rules in failing to make proper disclosure of the side-letter arrangements, nor did the non-disclosure have the effect that any of the registered players were ineligible to play, and for this and other reasons no sporting sanction or penalty should be imposed on

Rangers FC." A fine of £250,000, however, was imposed for the non-disclosure of side-letters issued to players revealing the details of the EBTs, but this was applied to oldco.

Ally McCoist spoke eloquently when the verdict was announced. He said, "I think the result of the Commission has totally vindicated the entire club and the playing staff throughout that period. We always felt and hoped it would be the case and it goes without saying that we are delighted with the outcome. We feel that common sense has prevailed, thankfully. It's been niggling away at all our minds for a long time now, and it has been the same for players and ex-players and certainly supporters.

"It was worrying because we always hoped for the right outcome, but you never know. It's great that we have some closure on it now. We were 100 per cent sure in our own minds that there had been no wrong-doing in terms of trying to seek an unfair advantage, or to say it more bluntly, cheat, because

Rangers only had a minimal presence at Tannadice with Charles Green, non-executive director Ian Hart and Head of Football Administration Andrew Dickson representing the club. Director of Communications Jim Traynor was in the background.

that is the worst crime you can ever level at a sportsman. To have something like that levelled at you is pretty outrageous and I'm thrilled for all the fans, for the staff and all the players that a sensible outcome has been reached."

The manager reiterated the importance of Rangers' victories in the last decade when he said, "These titles were won on the park. You set out at the start of every season to win the title and I think it was unanimous from every ex-player writing in the newspapers that there was no unfair advantage being sought during this period. I'm just hopeful we can put this saga behind us. We have come a long way but this cloud was hanging over us. Now it has gone and we can move forward.

"I have spoken to supporters who haven't slept at night – that's how much it means to them. We take satisfaction with what we feel is the correct result but now it's time for us to move on as a club. The recovery has started and we want to continue our efforts to get the club back to where we want to get to."

So despite months of vitriol from certain quarters and undeniable leaks from government offices, Rangers had been vindicated on two counts. There was no tax liable on the vast majority of the EBTs and they did not give them a sporting advantage on the field.

Sadly, on 4 February HMRC announced it was to appeal the First Tier Tax Tribunal verdict, which ruled that tax was not liable, and Charles Green quite rightly highlighted the futility of this course of action. He said, "All Rangers fans welcomed the First Tier Tax Tribunal verdict last November and will be disappointed that HMRC have now launched an appeal against their judgement. The ruling of the First Tier Tax Tribunal does not affect the operations and the financial position of the club as it stands today and the appeal will have no effect on us, as this is an historic case for The Rangers Football Club plc ['oldco'].

"As HMRC stated last June when they decided to vote against the proposed 'oldco' CVA, no tax liabilities relating to 'oldco' would transfer across to the new company. HMRC have also reaffirmed this position to the club's tax advisers, Deloitte. What the appeal does do, however, is cast a cloud of uncertainty and confusion over a situation that has already been ruled on and has taken a number of years to investigate.

"There is no money to be gained by HMRC, as the old company has been liquidated, so you have to ask why they are pursuing the matter further when the original EBT enquiry took years to reach a conclusion. I have written in the strongest possible terms to HMRC pointing out the futility of such an appeal."

On the field February was a much better month, as Rangers produced three successive victories in the league which underlined the fact that they would win the SFL 3 championship at a canter. They recovered from the bitter disappointment of Tannadice with a comfortable 4–0 victory over Queen's Park at Ibrox on 9 February when Ian Black scored his first gaol for the club, Dean Shiels netted and Andy Little scored twice to maintain his impressive strike rate for the season.

A week later Little was at it again with two more goals in a 4–1 demolition of Clyde at Broadwood, while David Templeton also scored two magnificent goals, the first of which – a ferocious drive from outside the penalty area – was later voted goal of the season. He said, "My first goal got me out of a hole because I felt I wasn't doing well enough. Even the simple things were not coming off for me. But that strike rekindled my confidence and I felt I played a lot better in the second half.

"I was pleased with my second goal, too. The ball broke to me on the edge of the box and I was going to take it on my right but the defender shoved me onto my left and I managed to strike it well into the far corner.

Dean Shiels was also in on the goal action against Queen's Park in a victory which gave the Ibrox men a 22-point lead at the top of the table.

"Three points was the main thing, but we managed to get a few good goals too so I think everyone was pleased with the performance."

Rangers were back down in Berwick on 23 February, and despite losing a goal in five minutes when Darren Lavery's header clipped Anestis Argyriou on its way into the net, they went on to win 3–1 at Shielfield Park. Dean Shiels brought Rangers level from the penalty spot then Little produced a stunning volley from Lee Wallace's cross to make it 2–1, before Seb Faure netted his first goal for the club twenty minutes into the second half.

Strangely Rangers had problems in their final match of the month when they were held 1–1 by Stirling Albion, who had beaten them at Forthbank earlier in the season. Little scored another fine goal but the Light Blues sloppily lost an equaliser to a set-piece. It was a stumble but it mattered little in the grand scheme of things as Rangers took a 20-point lead into the month of March.

There is no doubt that the influx of young players into the first team in the 2012/13 campaign was one of the highlights and Ally McCoist continued to secure the best ones on longer team deals. Kal Naismith, Chris Hegarty and goalkeeper Scott Gallacher all signed two-year deals, as did defender Kyle McAusland, who spent the 2012/13 season on loan at Ayr United, while exciting young Canadian Fraser Aird put pen to paper on a five-year contract.

Aird had played a key role in the SFL Reserve League campaign and he was a key protagonist as the young Rangers side lifted the trophy on their final match of the season when they defeated Queen's Park in front of a healthy crowd at Ibrox. Tommy Wilson's side had been chasing Morton for most of the campaign but goals from Aird and fellow Canuck Luca Gasparotto took them to the title, and captain Andy Mitchell proudly lifted the trophy. The events were not lost on Aird,

The players were wrapped up as they braved the elements.

whose Toronto-based father Bill is a lifelong fan. He said, "Sitting at home last summer I didn't even think I would have had a chance in the first team, so to do as well as I have done and land a five-year deal was brilliant. I never really imagined that day would come, to be honest, but training with the boys every day and making appearances was great.

"The Reserves were brilliant for the boys who were not playing many games because it gave us an opportunity to impress the gaffer. It was by playing well in the Reserves earlier in the season that I got my chance with the first team.

Hopefully that will be me here for quite a while, and I'll be delighted to be here for as long as I can."

It had been a good month all round for Rangers as they achieved success on and off the field, with the SPL Commission verdict vindicating the club's use of EBTs and a string of victories giving them what was effectively an unassailable lead. The key was to go on and complete the main target of the 2012/13 season and that was the clinching of the SFL 3 title, but that was going to prove a little more difficult than it seemed.

Top left: Andy Little relished the main striking role against Clyde on 16 February and fired Rangers into the lead after only eight minutes.

Top right: The Ulsterman made it twenty for the season with a fantastic left-foot finish which flew high into the net.

Bottom left: David Templeton then took over and smashed a sensational twenty-five-yard strike, which was later voted Rangers goal of the season.

Bottom right: The former Hearts man scored an equally impressive second goal with his left foot in the second half as Rangers ran out 4–1 winners.

Chris HEGARTY 2

Top far left: Ally McCoist knew it was important to tie down the better younger players and front player Kal Naismith was given a two-year deal.

Bottom far left: Young Canadian Fraser Aird may have only played a handful of matches in the first team but Rangers felt his potential was worth a five-year investment. Ally McCoist and Aird celebrated the deal on 15 February.

Top left: Chris Hegarty was one of the first players to commit to Rangers during the turbulence of the summer of 2012 and he was rewarded with a two-year contract in February.

Bottom left: Acting captain Lee Wallace led Rangers onto the field at Forthbank Stadium from the cramped tunnel area for another clash with Stirling Albion which proved to be problematic.

Above: The striking prowess of Andy Little was on display again at Forthbank on 26 February with a smooth finish which gave Rangers the lead.

Top right: David Templeton was quick to congratulate the striker who had been on deadly form again in the month of February.

Bottom right: It all went south for Rangers, however, as Albion produced an equaliser when Ross Forsyth (No.3) headed home from close range and it finished 1–1.

Above: To win the SFL Reserve championship was a fantastic achievement for all of the young players at Murray Park and another feather in the cap for the coaching staff in the youth department.

Top left: The Rangers reserves went for glory in their final league match of the season against Queen's Park and Fraser Aird fired them into the lead with an excellent right-foot strike.

Bottom left: Fellow Canadian Luca Gasparotto powered in a header for the second goal and that took the young Rangers men to the title.

Chapter 9
Slow March to the Title

THERE WAS perhaps an inevitability that given the mayhem and madness that Rangers had endured in the previous eighteen months there would be nothing simple about being crowned champions of SFL 3. It was not so much a charge to the title as a slow march, and in the end Rangers were officially title winners on 30 March while travelling on the team bus between Montrose and Glasgow, when it was revealed that Queen's Park had been beaten by Elgin City. The Light Blues had drawn 0–0 at Links Parks, which had followed another stalemate the previous week at home to bogey team Stirling Albion, so it was more of a stutter than a sprint to glory – but they got there in the end.

In mitigation, Rangers were so far in front of the rest that they naturally switched off a little bit but they managed to enjoy themselves when the title was finally theirs. The news came through that it was all over when the team bus was near Aberuthven, which is close to Gleneagles, and boss Ally McCoist ordered a detour to the village so the players could have a celebratory drink.

McCoist said, "It was hilarious. We stopped off right on the final whistle of the Queen's Park-Elgin game, when we knew we had won the title. As you can imagine, we walked in and some of the lads are still only old enough to drink lemonades. But when we got into the pub, there were two punters at the bar and they quickly shouted to the owner of the place to remind him of his strict rules about having no football colours!

"With twenty Rangers players standing there in their tracksuits, it was very funny and we stopped there for half an hour or so for the boys to have a celebratory drink which was well earned.

"I've got to tell you that one of the best moments of my season was around 4.20pm when it came on the radio that Elgin City had been awarded a penalty. The roar that went up from the back of the bus was fantastic, and the punters should know that. It was equalled when we heard they had converted the penalty and then when the final whistle went. Make no mistake, it meant so much to the players. I'm really happy for them."

That moment from the Hampden game stirred everyone on the bus, as the players were feeling a bit down after the flat performance at Montrose. Chris Hegarty revealed, "Everything was doom and gloom. The 0–0 draw felt like a defeat and there weren't many happy faces on the bus. At first we hadn't thought much about Queen's Park. Then the radio went on just as Elgin scored.

The Rangers players and coaching staff celebrated their SFL 3 title back at the Auchenhowie training centre after learning they had become champions on the bus back from Montrose.

Everyone started cheering and there was a bit of life about us. The banter started flowing again. It was a brilliant feeling, and when the final result eventually came in, the lads were bouncing.

"For most of us it was our first medal. Only Lee McCulloch and Neil Alexander had won medals at Rangers before. To do it after such a hard season and everything the club had been through was great and we won it with five games to spare.

"We stopped at a wee pub, which was brilliant. We all went in to have 'one for the road' and there was real excitement. We were all jumping about, but the people in the bar were great with us. We were celebrating a title win in a pub the size of your living room.

"We were all packed in and later I went outside to phone my mum and dad back home. They were over the moon for me. Everyone was as high as kites. On the bus we were all shaking each other's hands and hugging each other. The gaffer was delighted, as was Ian Durrant, Kenny McDowall and Jim Stewart. It was a special feeling all the way back knowing we had won the division."

The players returned to Murray Park, where they posed for official pictures to celebrate their win and it was probably a relief to many that they had finally made it over the line after a tough month.

It had all started quite well when the Light Blues ran out 3–1 winners over East Stirlingshire on 2 March when captain Lee McCulloch returned from injury and was an inspiration

on the day. In keeping with the often-obtuse nature of the season, Rangers were a goal down at half-time but they won comfortably in the second half, with Andy Little scoring twice and McCulloch netting on his return. There was also a very welcome spectator in the directors' box that day in the shape of Sandy Jardine, who addressed the fans over the PA system before kick-off to thank them for their support as he continued his treatment for cancer. It was another very bright moment in a very bright period for Rangers, as they had just announced two commercial deals with the news coming hot on the heels of the SPL Commission verdict into EBTs. A five-year kit deal with Puma was revealed and it was also announced that Blackthorn Cider would be the shirt sponsors for the 2013/14 season, so more revenue was being created.

On 4 March the interim financial results were released and they revealed that Rangers had generated £9.5 million in revenue but posted a loss of £7 million in the period May to December 2012. Much of this was due to virtually no revenue coming in during the summer and the costs associated with the takeover, including paying off football debts, most of which would not recur. Certainly finance director Brian Stockbridge was very encouraged that the turnover of the club could be greatly increased in the years ahead, especially with the deals in place with Sports Direct and Puma. He said, "When Rangers did its own retail it made £20.5 million turnover and £5.6 million profit just from merchandising. But because the club needed money, it gave it to JJB and took an upfront payment, then took the £3 million annual licensing fee. So, let's say if we can only do as good as £20 million with Mike Ashley as our partner, with Puma and with Internet sales, then suddenly we are looking at £80 million to £90 million turnover. Then you look at the additional sponsorship possibilities and think it would be nice to get it to £100 million, but even then I wouldn't think my job would be done at that point, as it could go on beyond that.

Top left: It was a special moment for captain Lee McCulloch to lead the team to success.

Bottom left: The skipper had his game face on as he shook hands with referee Brian Colvin.

Top right: Andy Little fired in his first goal against the Shire after they had taken a shock lead at Ibrox on 2 March.

Top far right: It's a second goal for Andy Little as he put Rangers ahead against the bottom-placed club.

Right: Skipper McCulloch made a comeback to remember when he netted the third goal on his return to the side to secure a 3–1 win.

"The Puma deal is a very good one. Typically, a manufacturer pays upfront and will claw that back at the end through the shirt prices. With Puma, I negotiated that we get a very high royalty rate on everything, even what we sell in the shop here at Ibrox."

While the financial prospects looked good, the football results were not too clever, not least a dismal home defeat by Annan Athletic on 9 March when the Galabank side stunned Ibrox by winning 2–1. Again, in another set of circumstances this would be viewed as an appalling result – perhaps the worst in history – but it is hard to quantify given the situation Rangers were in and the standard they were at. Rangers were two down before Andy Little bundled in a counter and they were unable to find any more goals, much to the horror of the home fans. To add injury to insult, Dean Shiels was carried off with medial ligament damage and did not play again in the campaign. A week later it was a bit of a slog at Elgin but Rangers were never in any danger and won the game 1–0, thanks to a Lee McCulloch penalty.

Kevin Kyle was released from his contract on 16 March after a mutual agreement was reached with the big striker, who had been troubled by a bad ankle injury since the Montrose game on 15 December. However, there was a much more serious matter for fellow striker Fran Sandaza. He had been duped by a prank phone-caller and revealed details of his contract as well as a desire to potentially move to another club, and the conversation was posted on the Internet.

Sandaza was suspended by the club on 22 March and on 3 April it was announced that his contract was being terminated for what the club believed to be a material breach of his contract of employment. It was another unusual twist to the remarkable story of Rangers in the Third Division, although most connected with the club are so battle-hardened that they have come to expect the unexpected.

Overall, first-team coach Ian Durrant knew that the month of March was not a great one in terms of the quality of the football, but he emphasised that it was all about achieving the ultimate aim. He said, "It had been a topsy-turvy month and in the end the point at Montrose was enough for us with Queen's Park losing later that day. It was a great celebration coming down the road on the bus. When you win a league you should celebrate no matter what league it is. We had worked hard to get to that point and I think some nerves kicked in the closer we got to winning the title. But that's what we set out to do at the start of the season so we achieved our main aim.

"We started the month well with a 3–1 win over East Stirling, although it was all about the second half that day. We were one down at the break and we asked them to up it a gear and they responded. With Andy Little and big Jig up front you always have a chance and that partnership paid dividends again, with Andy grabbing two and Jig netting the other one. It was well set up by David Templeton, who played him in, and Lee finished very well.

"The Annan game was obviously a huge disappointment. No disrespect to them and they took their chances, but it was a poor day for us. We had a lot of possession but we couldn't do anything with it and we let a lot of people down that day.

"Up at Elgin if we had put our chances away in the first fifteen minutes we would have been out of sight, but we needed a penalty to make sure of the win and our most experienced player obliged. It doesn't look a great score-line but we were comfortable throughout the game.

"I think nerves played a part in the game with Stirling Albion. We were just trying to urge them over the line, but it wasn't to be. Similarly if we had scored early in that game it would have been comfortable."

It might not have been pretty, but the main target for the season had been achieved. Rangers were champions.

Left: Rangers went through their final pre-match preparations before heading down the Ibrox tunnel to take on Annan Athletic on 9 March. It was not a day they are likely to remember.

Above: Annan centre-back Steven Swinglehurst smashed into Dean Shiels as he challenged for the ball, taking the Rangers player out in the process.

Top right: The tackle by Swinglehurst ended Shiels' season as he suffered serious ligament damage to his knee, which had to be put into a brace to aid the recovery.

Right: It was a nightmarish day for Rangers as Annan celebrated an historic 2–1 victory at Ibrox when the Light Blues succumbed to their first home defeat of the season.

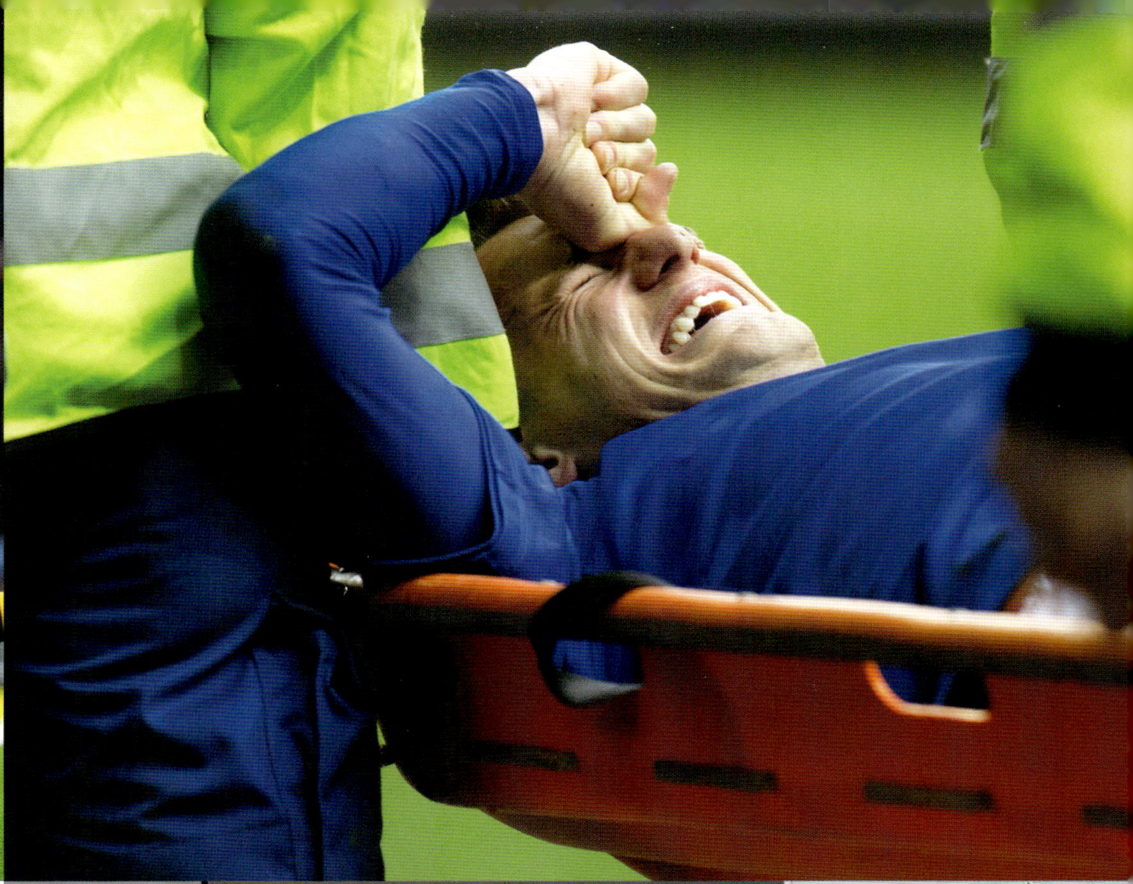

Press Association

The Journey continued north again on 16 March when Rangers travelled
to face Elgin City for the second time at their Borough Briggs ground.

Press Association

It was a tight match with Elgin, although Rangers were never in any danger, and this Lee McCulloch penalty was enough to separate the sides.

The Rangers players always get behind the Lucky Bluenose Day campaign that raises money for the Charity Foundation, with Kane Hemmings, Robbie Crawford, Kyle Hutton and Lee McCulloch all game for a laugh.

Lee Wallace looked a bit serious as he donned the Bluenose, but Kal Naismith and Seb Faure were having fun.

Young guns Fraser Aird, Chris Hegarty and Andy Mitchell got in on the act.

Without prompting, Greek defender Anestis Argyriou got right into the spirit of things.

These fans also showed their support on 23 March at the Stirling Albion game.

Opposite top: It wasn't great viewing for manager Ally McCoist as once again Stirling, who took four points from Rangers at home, caused the Ibrox men a problem.

Far left: Rangers were held to a goal-less draw by Albion but one positive was the first start of the season by Kane Hemmings, who had been on loan for two months with Cowdenbeath.

Middle left: This young fan did not see a lot to get excited about at Montrose – even if he was looking through blue-tinted glasses.

Left: David Templeton did his best to inspire the team at Montrose, but for the second week running Rangers suffered a stalemate.

Above: A wide shot of Links Park on 30 March where Rangers were hoping to clinch the SFL 3 title. In the end the point they secured at Montrose was enough as Queen's Park lost at home to Elgin.

This scarf belongs to lifelong fan Agnes Douglas from Motherwell, who was wearing it at Montrose on 30 March when Rangers eventually sealed the title. She started collecting badges in 2005 and now has two scarves full of them.

Chapter 10
All Change at the Top

WITH PHASE ONE of the Journey completed the coaching staff at Rangers had hoped that they could now firmly focus on a more stable future and begin making their plans for the continued recovery. On the field they felt that the players would be more relaxed and could finish the season with a flourish and they could also concentrate on trying to bolster the squad for the new season. However, in keeping with the upheaval that has followed the club in the past two years, there were big changes at the top, and by the end of the month both Charles Green and close colleague Imran Ahmad had left the club and one of the original investors, Craig Mather, was made chief operating officer as well as interim chief executive.

The board had been troubled by media reports which centred on the takeover process and the subsequent running of the club, and they ordered an independent inquiry. They were also concerned with comments made by Green about Ahmad, which were perceived in certain quarters to be ill advised at best and potentially racist. A statement read: "The board has announced it is to commission an independent examination and report in view of recent allegations in the media concerning the chief executive, Charles Green, the commercial director, Imran Ahmad, and their management of the club.

"The decision to commission the examination was taken unanimously by those in attendance at today's meeting including non-executive and executive directors. The independent report will be commissioned and completed as speedily as possible and presented directly to the non-executive directors of the company.

"The chief executive will not be involved in the conduct of the examination. The board wishes to make clear that it is not prejudging any of the issues involved and that the object of this exercise is to clarify the situation to the satisfaction of shareholders, supporters, staff and board members.

"Instructions recently given to lawyers in England and Scotland with a view to taking legal action to challenge these recent allegations will form part of the independent examination.

"Also at today's meeting, the chief executive of the club apologised unreservedly to board members and the wider Rangers support for any offence caused by remarks he made in an interview last week regarding Imran Ahmad.

"Mr Green told the board that in trying to make a point in the interview that, as chief executive, he would not countenance any form of prejudice towards

Top: There was an empty seat beside director Ian Hart and Head of Football Administration Andrew Dickson at the home game with Peterhead on 20 April following the resignation of Charles Green the day before.

Bottom: Craig Mather had been one of the original investors in the summer of 2012 and he was appointed interim chief executive of the club on 24 April.

The Rangers players met at Ibrox ahead of the short trip to Hampden to face Queen's Park on 7 April, where they enjoyed a hearty breakfast and – as ever – were well looked after by club stalwart Tiny Gallagher.

It gave the players the opportunity to relax a bit as they enjoyed their food and both David Templeton and Neil Alexander were amused by something.

The players get ready for the action against Queen's Park at Hampden on 7 April.

Kenny McDowall plotted for tactical planning for the Queen's Park game, as Ally McCoist looked on.

The assistant boss marked exactly what each player had to do at set-pieces, whether attacking or defending.

Ally McCoist explained to Emilson Cribari exactly what he wanted him to do in the match against Queen's.

employees or players at the club, he had exercised poor judgement in the words he chose. He apologised. The board accepted the explanation that there had been no intention to cause offence and accepted the chief executive's apology. The board is satisfied that the chief executive did not act in a racist manner but reminded him of the importance of all office bearers at Rangers upholding the standards expected by the club.

"Mr Green will deal with the pending SFA charge on this matter on a personal basis. The board wishes to reiterate Rangers is a club which is opposed to all forms of prejudice and has a long-established policy of working extensively in the community through a variety of programmes and initiatives to tackle issues such as racism and sectarianism."

Then on 19 April the dramatic news on Green broke when it was revealed that he was leaving his post as chief executive and would step down from the board at the end of May. A club statement read: "The Company announces that Charles Green has notified the board that he wishes to step down as chief executive with immediate effect. Recent weeks have seen media interest in the circumstances surrounding the period prior to the acquisition of the club by the consortium led by Mr Green.

"Whilst Mr Green strenuously denies any wrongdoing, he has recognised that this negative publicity is a distraction and is detracting from the achievements and reputation of the club. As a result, Mr Green has informed the board that he will leave his post with immediate effect and leave the Company, following an orderly handover, by the end of May.

"The board has commenced the search for a new chief executive and expects the role to attract high quality candidates from both within and outwith the industry. A further announcement will be made in due course."

Just two months earlier Green had said he expected to be with Rangers until he retired, but media reports linking him

Top: With the Hampden mission accomplished the players could relax on the team bus back to Ibrox.

Bottom left: Captain Lee McCulloch likes to relax in his own way by listening to music.

Bottom right: Fraser Aird is the same but he wins the cheesiest grin of the day competition.

with Craig Whyte meant that the fifty-nine-year-old opted to cut his ties after a quite extraordinary period in charge of the club.

On his departure he said, "Recent events have undoubtedly been a distraction for both myself and all involved with Rangers and I feel that it is appropriate that I step down so that the club can continue to progress back to where it belongs at the pinnacle of Scottish football.

"I am very proud to have been associated with a club of the stature of Rangers and am proud of the achievements of the club during my tenure as chief executive. My thanks go to the Rangers fans, whose support has been tremendous during my time at the club."

Chairman Malcolm Murray paid tribute to Green's efforts. He said, "Charles Green was instrumental in helping to secure financial stability for the club. The impact that he had in turning the club around from the dark days of last summer will never be forgotten by the fans who I am sure, like me, will thank him for this and for choosing to put the club ahead of his personal position at this time."

Green had undoubtedly been one of the most colourful characters ever seen in Scottish football, with a propensity to speak his mind, which worked well at times and drew scepticism on other occasions.

There was more drama when it was revealed on 27 April that Imran Ahmad had also left his position as commercial director with immediate effect, with the media reporting that he had been critical of Walter Smith and Ally McCoist when posting on a fans' website under a pseudonym.

Three days before this the board appointed Craig Mather to try and stabilise the situation. Chairman Malcolm Murray said, "We are very pleased to announce the appointment of Craig Mather as chief operating officer of Rangers. He will also be acting chief executive, which will allow us some time to

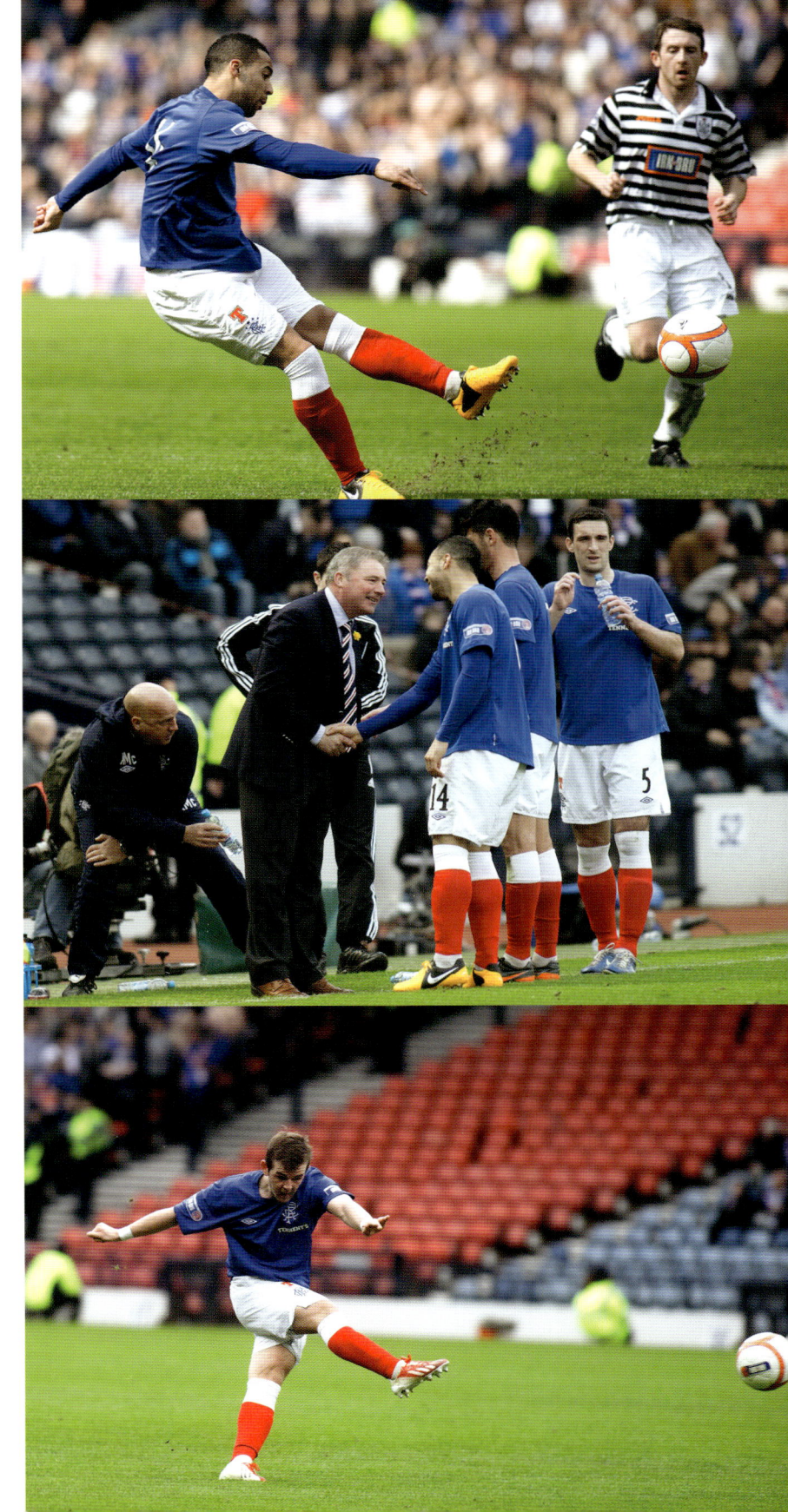

Top: Kane Hemmings grabbed his first senior Rangers goal in the 4–1 win over Queen's Park.

Middle: Boss Ally McCoist expressed his congratulations to the young striker for getting off the mark as a Rangers player.

Bottom: David Templeton fired in the second of his two goals against Queen's in the 4–1 win.

examine the credentials of candidates for this position on a permanent basis.

"Craig's appointment as chief operating officer will allow the company and the club to keep moving forward. Craig has invested £1 million of his own money in the club and is committed to playing an active part in delivering future success for Rangers. The board has approved his appointment and look forward to him pushing us in the correct direction. Craig will lead the business on a day-to-day basis, but I want to make it clear we are in a healthy position financially following the successful flotation of the company in December last year. I would also like to assure all of the supporters that this money is being used for the benefit of the club and nothing or no one else.

"The board has also instructed the law firm Pinsent Masons to conduct the investigation into alleged links between Craig Whyte and former and current personnel at the club. This process will be completed as swiftly as possible and no one should jump to conclusions regarding the outcome. The fans deserve to be reassured on clarity, transparency, asset ownership and this is the main purpose of the enquiry.

"The last week or so has been turbulent for the club but we should bear in mind that the process of rebuilding is well under way. Now is the time to move forward and the most important thing for all Rangers fans, myself included, is ensuring our club can play as constructive a part in Scottish football as possible."

Mather had been operating as Sporting Development Director, working regularly at Murray Park, so he already had an understanding of the operation. He said, "This is one of the world's great football clubs with a long

Opposite top left: Skipper McCulloch sent Rangers on the road to victory against Clyde with a good finish.

Opposite top right: Midfielder Kyle Hutton completed the job with only his second goal of the season.

Opposite bottom: He may be from La Plata in Argentina, but Hernán Pacheco is one of the most fanatical Rangers supporters you could meet. He regularly follows the team on RangersTV, but he was thrilled to visit Scotland with partner Carla and even more excited when the two of them were standard bearers at the Clyde game.

Left: The Rangers fans in the Broomloan Stand at the Clyde game on 13 April offered their own illustration of the task ahead with stage one of the Journey completed.

and proud history and I had no hesitation in investing personally in Rangers. My own business background is in sport and particularly in youth development, something that will be fundamental to the success of this club.

"Rangers fans have been outstanding in their support for the club during the most difficult of times and I know they don't know me and may have some doubts. I hope to dispel all of those if that is the case.

"I know there have been rumours about who is supposed to be connected with whom, but I prefer to distance myself from all of that. I know what my own hard

work has achieved over the years and where it has taken me, and I will use all of my experience and knowledge to help improve Rangers.

"I could not stand here and tell you I have always been a Rangers fan, but I can say, with profound honesty, that I have been around football all my life and I have known of Rangers and their huge successes for many years. But then, who hasn't?

"I am well aware of what this club means to so many people. I have been working at Rangers for the last year or so and the commitment and passion from the supporters

never ceases to amaze me. They deserve so much better than they've been getting of late. My job will be to make sure the work is put in to make them even prouder to be Rangers fans.

"It is incumbent on everyone working for Rangers that we make sure the club is in the best possible shape for next season and to create the platform on which fans can enthusiastically support the team."

Meanwhile, there was a major development in the league reconstruction saga when Ross County and St Mirren blocked the 12-12-18 proposal in a vote of the SPL clubs, rendering a vote among SFL clubs on the matter redundant. It seemed as though Rangers would get promotion after all.

Not for the first time football politics and corporate governance were topping the agenda, but Rangers still had matches to play and they made a good start to the month when they defeated Queen's Park 4–1 at Hampden on 7 April, with David Templeton hitting a double, Fraser Aird netting at the national stadium for the second time and Kane Hemmings grabbing his first goal of the season. A challenge match with good friends Linfield, who had come to Rangers' aid a year earlier by donating the proceeds of a match at Windsor Park, was staged at Ibrox on 10 April, and Chris Hegarty and youngster Andy Murdoch scored in a 2–0 Rangers win, which also included a debut for Canadian defender Luca Gasparotto. On 13 April a 2–0 win over Clyde was secured with goals from Lee McCulloch and Kyle Hutton, and then Rangers were stunned at home for the second time when Peterhead defeated them 2–1 on 20 April – and that was after McCulloch had put them in front. They finished the month with a far from convincing 4–2 win at Ochilview over East Stirlingshire in which Templeton scored another double – one from an excellent free kick – while Robbie Crawford and Ian Black were also on target.

There was one match to go and it would be the day that Rangers would be able to celebrate their efforts for the campaign overall when they received the SFL 3 trophy.

Opposite top: Ian Black did not look too impressed but he surely was as David Templeton curled a terrific free-kick into the East Stirlingshire net for the second goal in what was a 4–2 win. Templeton also scored the fourth from close range.

Opposite bottom left: Black managed to get in on the goal action too, with the third in what was the final match of the month on 27 April.

Opposite bottom right: One of new chief executive Craig Mather's first tasks was to head to Ochilview with Finance Director Brian Stockbridge for the penultimate match of the season on 27 April.

Top right: The annual Player of the Year awards at Glasgow's Hilton Hotel on 28 April were a runaway success, and even though Lewis Macleod missed four months of the season, he was the pick for Young Player of the Year.

Bottom right: The exceptional efforts of Sandy Jardine, particularly during the awful days of 2012, meant that he was the obvious recipient of the John Greig Achievement Award and Ally McCoist happily collected it on his behalf.

PLAYER OF THE YEAR 2013
McEwan Fraser Legal
Solicitors & Estate Agents

McEwan Fraser Legal
PLAYER OF THE YEAR 2013

PLAYER OF THE YEAR 2013
McEwan Fraser Legal
Solicitors & Estate Agents

RANGERS FOOTBALL CLUB
READY
McEwan Fraser Legal
Solicitors & Estate Agents

Opposite top left: David Templeton hit the target fifteen times during the campaign, and it was his sensational first goal against Clyde on 16 February that was voted goal of the season.

Opposite top right: It was a proud moment for Ulsterman Andy Little to win the Sam English Bowl for finishing top league goal-scorer.

Opposite bottom left: It's always great to be respected by your peers and Lee Wallace was thrilled to be named Players' Player of the Year.

Opposite bottom right: There were a lot of top performers in 2012/13 but Lee McCulloch was an inspiration with his performances, his goals, his versatility and his leadership and was the obvious choice for Player of the Year.

Above: The youth department enjoyed another big success when the Under-17s defeated Celtic 3–2 in the Glasgow Cup Final at Firhill in front of 6,500 fans, with Junior Ogen (2) and Ryan Hardie scoring the goals.

The squad that won the SFL 3 title.

Back (left to right): Davie Lavery (masseur), Chris Hegarty, Ross Perry, Emilson Cribari, Lee Wallace, Kal Naismith, Kyle Hutton, Steve Walker (physiotherapist) and Jimmy Bell (kit controller).

Middle: Gary Sherriff (sports scientist), Darren Cole, Anestis Argyriou, Sébastien Faure, Neil Alexander, Scott Gallacher, Lee McCulloch, Andy Little, Kane Hemmings and Steve Harvey (video analysis).

Front: Adam Owen (head of sports science), David Templeton, Robbie Crawford, Lewis Macleod, Kenny McDowall, Ally McCoist, Ian Durrant, Fraser Aird, Ian Black, Andy Mitchell and Jim Stewart (goalkeeping coach).

Chapter 11
Silver Lining

AN ASTONISHING 50,048 crowd – another new world record for a fourth-tier league match – packed out Ibrox on 4 May to witness the tangible reward for the most extraordinary campaign in Rangers' history. The match with Berwick Rangers was largely forgettable, other than the Fraser Aird header that separated the sides and gave Rangers a 1–0 victory, which meant they finished 24 points clear of their closest challengers, Peterhead. It was all about the post-match pomp and ceremony, and there was an almighty roar when captain Lee McCulloch stepped onto the Irn-Bru podium to join his teammates and lift the SFL 3 trophy.

The scenes were joyous and carefree. For a period the horrors of the previous year were forgotten as players and supporters celebrated with great gusto, and they undoubtedly deserved these moments. It perhaps seems odd that a club of Rangers' stature should make such a meal of winning the lowest honour in the Scottish game, but everything has to be put into context. There might not have been a football club at all. Flags waved, fans sang their hearts out and the confetti flew into the air. It was a day of celebration and even for someone who has achieved such greatness in the game, it was a day never to forget for manager Ally McCoist. He said, "It was great. I watched big Jig go up and lift the trophy and it was just brilliant. When the supporters saw him do that they knew that was stage one completed. The reaction from the crowd was everything I hoped it would be.

"We have won the league, and it was all about the supporters. They deserve unbelievable thanks and praise from everyone within our football club. I said it out on the park and I genuinely meant it that if it wasn't for them there wouldn't be a Rangers Football Club. They've been truly wonderful. It's just brilliant to see the young boys in the dressing room and for a lot of them it was the first thing they have won. To do it in front of over 50,000 fans was incredible and whatever they do in the rest of their lives they will never forget that. I said to them they should cherish it but I am very hopeful a lot of them will go on to win a lot more. Once you have enjoyed a bit of success there is no doubt you want more of it and I hope our boys can go on and do that again and again."

It was fitting that McCulloch should be the man to spark the celebrations, having shown great loyalty to remain with the club when so many other first-team players walked out and deserted Rangers the previous summer. He said,

It was the moment Lee McCulloch had been waiting for as he joyfully lifted the SFL 3 trophy to spark scenes of great celebration at Ibrox on 4 May.

Opposite top: The home dressing room was eerily still with the kit laid out perfectly for the final game. It would be rather messy after the game!

Opposite bottom left: Even though there was a title party coming, there was still some work to be done, and Ian Durrant set out the tactics ahead of the game with Berwick.

Opposite bottom right: The captain showed off the trophy with Kane Hemmings, Andy Little and Andy Mitchell.

Right: Lee McCulloch had often wondered what it was like to lift a trophy as Rangers captain, and the experience did not let him down.

"Going up there to get the trophy was just unbelievable, especially as captain. It meant so much to me and also my family as well.

"I've seen previous captains lift league trophies, such as big Davie [Weir] and Barry [Ferguson], and I wondered how it would feel to do that at the end of a season. I now know and it's amazing, it really is. My boy was a mascot for the game and my mum and dad came along as well. They don't get to a lot of games but I know it was a proud moment for them.

"Overall it was a fantastic day and again I would like to thank all the fans for setting a world record with the crowd and creating a wonderful atmosphere, especially at the end. We can now look forward to the summer and come back refreshed and ready for the next step."

There was even more fun and enjoyment for the fans two days later when a Legends match was staged against Manchester United which benefitted the Rangers Charity Foundation and UNICEF. The great Rangers players of the past rolled back the years as they defeated United 4–1 and, incredibly, the greatest goal-scorer of them all – McCoist – scored twice, while Jörg Albertz smashed a trademark howitzer and Alex Rae netted a terrific fourth goal. It added to the feel-good factor around the club and it brought the curtain down on the playing side of things in the most enjoyable way.

It had been a season like no other. Everything was new, from the level of player the coaches were working with to the grounds they had to travel to amid the same levels of expectation from an unbelievable support. Every opposing team, it seemed, treated their meetings with Rangers as if their lives depended on it, not only in a physical way but also in terms of level of performance. They wanted to play to their best against Rangers and that brought its own difficulties.

It was like the Rangers of old – the star-studded one that recently won three successive SPL titles – playing thirty-six

Top left: The beer and the champagne were flowing in the Ibrox dressing room as the squad savoured their success.

Top right: It was a day to remember for Kyle Hutton and David Templeton, as they won their first honours for Rangers.

Above left: Ally McCoist and Kenny McDowall were the main cheerleaders as the celebrations really got going.

Above right: Lewis Macleod was proud of his contribution to the 2012/13 campaign, as Kyle Hutton looked on.

Right: The Ulster trio of Andy Little, Dean Shiels and Andy Mitchell were thrilled to be part of it all.

Top: Rangers won the final match of the season against Berwick 1–0, and it was Fraser Aird who decided it with a diving header.

Bottom: It was a fantastic moment for Aird and it meant that Rangers finished 24 points clear of their nearest challengers.

Scottish Cup ties against organised and motivated smaller clubs. The only thing was that this was not the Rangers of old. It was a thrown-together squad where there was no option but to flood the team with young players who, in normal circumstances, would only have been used sporadically at best. That led to performances which were not as polished as they might have been. Indeed, in all honesty some were quite wretched, particularly in the early sojourns around the country and latterly when the team had such a commanding lead and was just trying to get over the line.

However, Ally McCoist was proud of the achievement and he enjoyed most of it too. He said, "SFL 3 was a brilliant experience for us all. It was as difficult as we expected it to be – even if others didn't share the same view. Many of the places we went to were difficult to play at because of the environment, the excitement surrounding the game and the way the teams played against us. However, we got used to it and more often than not we conquered it. We had a couple of blips near the end of the season, but generally the home results were good for us and that gave us the foundation in the league campaign. Equally, we found a winning run away from home and that took us to our target, which was winning the league. I know that the supporters have enjoyed the trips and we did too because we were made so welcome by all of the other clubs. They were very hospitable.

"Overall our boys deserve enormous credit because they went out there and got the results and won the title. We patched together a team with some signings and players from the youth academy with no experience and we knew they wouldn't get any credit but we certainly know what they did, and they all get a big pat on the back from us."

Of course there were highlights on the field. Even though it was a different level, between them Andy Little and Lee McCulloch scored fifty-one goals, and that tally had not been

Left: It had been a long and sometimes bumpy road for Ally McCoist, but the reward was championship success.

Top right: The Berwick players and the match officials formed a guard of honour to welcome the champions onto the field for the final game.

Bottom right: Ally McCoist and Ian Durrant have been in this pose many times before and winning SFL 3 meant as much as all of their previous triumphs.

reached since McCoist and Mark Hateley terrorised Scottish defences in the 1990s. Lewis Macleod emerged as a real talent in midfield and there were very encouraging signs from Barrie McKay, Robbie Crawford and Fraser Aird. Neil Alexander's experience was vital, while Lee Wallace was a solid, dependable performer. David Templeton scored some stunning goals and set up almost as many. Each and every one of the younger players had good moments and undoubtedly gained valuable experience that will stand them in good stead.

McCoist added, "There were some big bright points – obviously the goals from McCulloch and Little, the breakthrough of younger boys like Macleod, McKay, Crawford, Aird and latterly Luca Gasparotto. There were also solid performances from our goalkeeper, Neil, and Lee Wallace, so there were many pluses for us.

"I would hope that the experience of this season would stand all the boys in good stead for next season. It won't be a shock for us to go to venues like the ones we have just experienced because there is no doubt that it was like that in SFL 3. So that should stand us in good stead for next season when we will be going to similar places."

Of course the journeys were eventful for the supporters and were hugely beneficial to the host clubs, who maximised the visits of Rangers and considerably increased their revenues as a result. Some trips were a little more awkward than others as the Rangers team bus racked up close to 4,000 miles travelling the length and breadth of the country.

McCoist said, "We have met some great characters and it's been wonderful, and I would like to think we have returned the hospitality. I have read stats that our two visits to some of the clubs we played is equivalent to revenue for nearly a whole season, so we are delighted to have helped in that regard. We had some scrapes too. A tree fell down across the road as we tried to make our way home from Elgin in

December. I'm still not sure if that was pre-arranged because we were not too good up there that day! We have had to take detours on country roads and gone past lochs that I have never seen on a map before. Our bus driver, Gregg, has taken left turns when it should have been right, but I'll let him off because he's been great all season and he deserves a special mention. I'm sure at one stage we saw a sign that said twenty miles to Reykjavik, but it has been a wonderful experience for all of us."

Of course, while success was achieved on the field there remain difficulties within the operational structure of the club in terms of developments within the boardroom and McCoist, like all supporters, sincerely hopes that a stable path can be found. He said, "It's not been fair on the staff and the supporters. All we have wanted was a bit of reassurance and to get into a position that we could build from. Sadly I don't think we are there yet because there are still one or two changes going on and to an extent that is natural.

"I would cry out and hope for stability so we can have a real opportunity to move on. The most important thing is the fans want to see a winning team. They got that with the team winning SFL 3 and now we move to the next step."

Overall, it was an extraordinary year for McCoist, who had to fire-fight questioning on off-the-field matters with remarkable regularity and at the same time try to complete the task on the field of play. He concluded, "I guess it's for others to say how I have handled it, but I will say that my job has probably been quite different to most managers' jobs in the country.

"I have been to press conferences where I haven't been asked a question about football. So it's not ideal. All a manager or coach wants to do is talk about his team and forthcoming matches. I want to develop and grow as a manager and I want to take Rangers to the top places. So I hope that in the coming years I will get the opportunity to do that."

Part one of the Journey is completed. Now for part two.

These fans decided to go down the patriotic route as they joined in the title celebrations.

It was a day to have fun, paint your face and wear a spikey red, white and blue wig!

The jesters' hats were out too as supporters of all ages got into the carnival atmosphere.

It's not clear if Cochise or Sitting Bull were Rangers supporters, but they had a representation at the title party.

This trio were getting wiggy with it as they lapped up the occasion at Ibrox.

Engraver Alan Smith from Robert Horn Jewellers got to work on the SFL 3 to make sure it was ready for the big day.

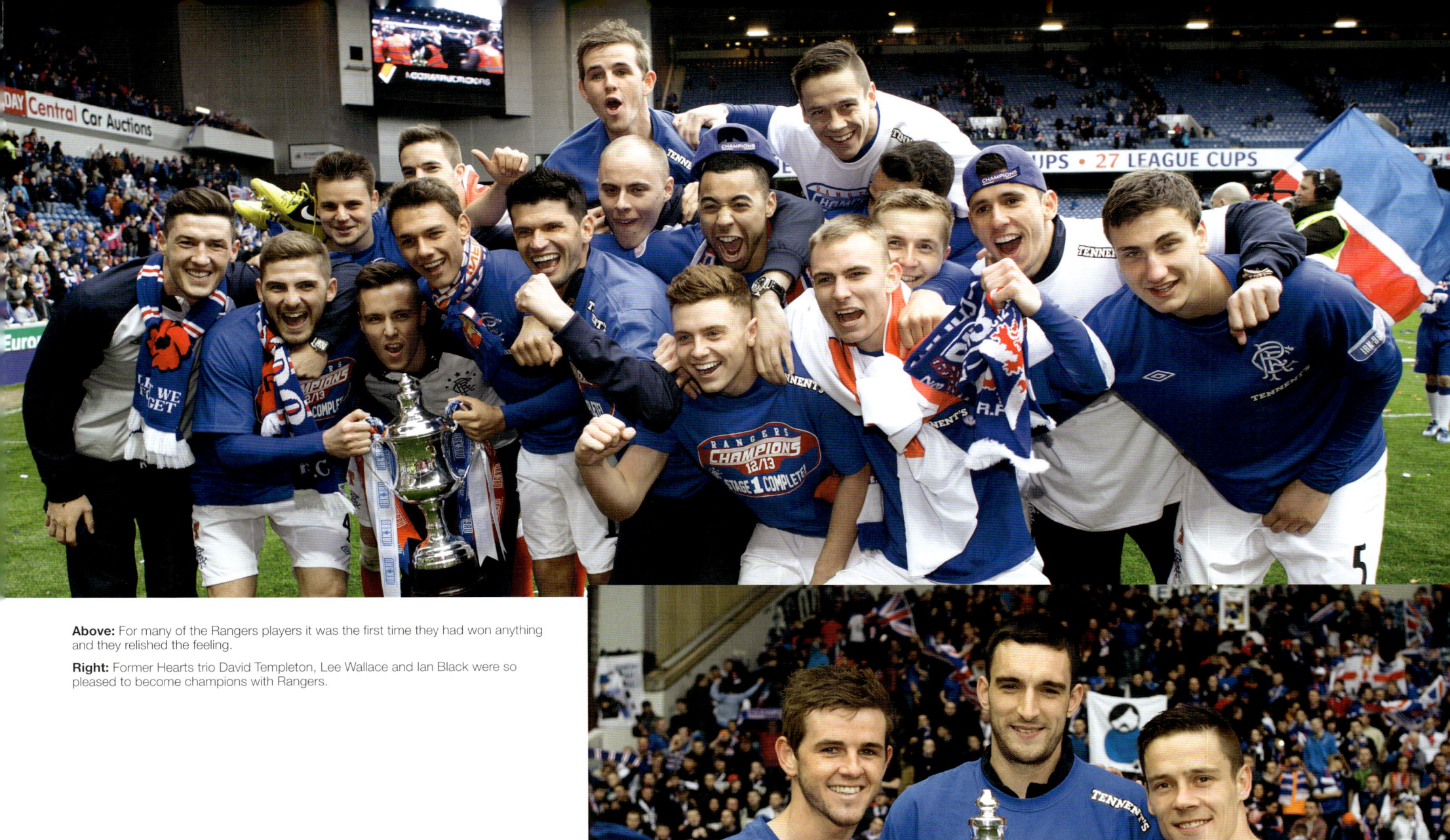

Above: For many of the Rangers players it was the first time they had won anything and they relished the feeling.

Right: Former Hearts trio David Templeton, Lee Wallace and Ian Black were so pleased to become champions with Rangers.

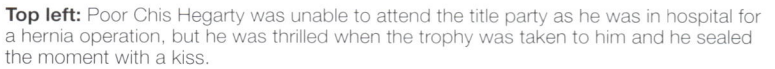

Top left: Poor Chis Hegarty was unable to attend the title party as he was in hospital for a hernia operation, but he was thrilled when the trophy was taken to him and he sealed the moment with a kiss.

Top right: There is little doubt that Andy Little was a top performer in the season with twenty-five goals so no wonder he cherished the moment on 4 May.

Left: It had been a whirlwind for teenage Canadian Fraser Aird, who scored some vital goals and penned a five-year deal to become a key part of Rangers' future.

Top: It was fantastic for the Ibrox fans to see such Rangers royalty as Stuart McCall, Lorenzo Amoruso, Jörg Albertz, Mark Hateley and Brian Laudrup, and the players really enjoyed it too.

Above: Sir Alex Ferguson was a special guest at the Legends game and there is no truth in the rumour that he resigned as Old Trafford boss two days later because Manchester United were beaten 4–1!

Right: Ally McCoist was back in the old routine as he blasted two goals in the wonderful Legends match which raised £75,000 for charity.

The Legends of Rangers and Manchester United put on a fantastic show
at Ibrox on 6 May to add to the feel-good factor that had been permeating
since the SFL 3 trophy lift two days earlier.